5/7/12

A HISTORY OF CRAIG GARDNER & CO.
THE FIRST 100 YEARS

Dublin in 1864, showing the proposed route of the Rathmines and Rathcoole Railway (a Craig Gardner client); note also the planned tunnel under the Liffey in place of the Butt Bridge loop line.
(From The Dublin Builder, 15 *June* 1864*)*

A view of Trinity Chambers, the firm's office for 100 years, by Muriel Brandt.

A HISTORY OF CRAIG GARDNER & CO.

THE FIRST 100 YEARS

TONY FARMAR

GILL AND MACMILLAN

Published in Ireland by
Gill and Macmillan Ltd
Goldenbridge
Dublin 8
with associated companies in
Auckland, Delhi, Gabarone, Hamburg, Harare,
Hong Kong, Johannesburg, Kuala Lumpur, Lagos,
London, Manzini, Melbourne, Mexico City,
Nairobi, New York, Singapore, Tokyo
© Craig Gardner & Co. 1988

Designed by Design Image, Dublin
Typeset in 11 on 13 Garamond by:
DISKON Technical Services Ltd, Dublin
Printed by Criterion Press Ltd, Dublin

All rights reserved. No part of this publication may be copied, reproduced or transmitted in any form or by any means, without permission of the publishers.

British Library of Congress Cataloguing in Publication Data

Farmar Tony
A History of Craig Gardner & Co.:
The First 100 Years
1. (Republic) Ireland. Accounting firms (Firm) Craig Gardner & Co., to 1968
I. Title
338.7'61657'09417

ISBN 0-7171-1594-1

CONTENTS

Preface
Acknowledgments
List of Illustrations
Introduction 1
1. The Very Beginning 5
2. Sole Practitioner, 1875-90 35
3. 'Auditors and Accountants', 1890-1904 61
4. Wider Horizons, 1904-24 87
5. Amalgamation with Mackie's, 1924-29 111
6. The 1930s and the Sweep 139
7. The Long Emergency of the 1940s 161
8. The Beginnings of Management 181
9. The Modern Firm 203
Appendix 1: Craig Gardner Partners,
           1866-1987 218
Appendix 2: Clients in the late 1890s 220
Appendix 3: The Allocation of Rooms
           in 1924 223
Appendix 4: Staff List, by Charging
           Grade, 1965 225
Index 229

PREFACE

In the year that Dublin celebrates its millennium and the Institute of Chartered Accountants in Ireland, whose first President was Robert Gardner, celebrates its centenary, it seems right that our firm, Craig Gardner & Co., should look to its own roots, which go back to the 1850s. Since that time our firm has had the good fortune to serve and be associated with an extraordinary range of personalities, organisations and events in the developing Irish community – business and social.

The firm's first 100 years, whose end, by happy chance, closely coincided with the move in 1968 from our original premises at the corner of Dame Street and Trinity Street to our offices in Ballsbridge, is the subject of this history. Much has changed since 1968, not least the fact that the firm has since then had to move premises again due to growth in both the size and scope of the practice and the need to have its physical facilities up-to-date and capable of supporting the new technologies now available to improve its client service capabilities.

I hope that readers of this book will enjoy it for what it is, namely, a glimpse of an aspect of Ireland during a century of great change from the 1860s to the 1960s. I and my partners look to the future with confidence as we, with our staff and clients, present and future, now create the material which will in time be the history of the second century of our firm, perhaps to be written some 80 years from now.

W. M. McCann, Senior Partner,
Craig Gardner & Co.
Dublin
March 1988

ACKNOWLEDGMENTS

In the course of writing even quite a short book such as this, many people have provided insights or information. Among those from Craig Gardner's past or present who provided most help were, in alphabetical order, Frank Belton, Paul Creedon, William Cunningham, John Blake Dillon, Des Hally, Marie Heade, William McCann, Noel MacMahon, Alan Molony, Gerard O'Brien, Heuston O'Neill, Maureen Quinn and Olive Vaughan.

The Institute's librarian, Eleanor Jenkins, was extremely helpful, as was her English counterpart, Michael Bywater, and Margaret Byrne of the Law Society. Dr Jean Archer, Dr Mary Daly, Dr David Dickson and Alex Findlater provided sources and background. Frank MacAuliffe and Gerry Keenan gave information on Clery's and P. J. Carroll respectively, and my thanks are due to Arnott's company secretary, John O'Sullivan, for allowing me access to Arnott's archives.

The illustrations on pages 9 and 79 were supplied courtesy of the Civic Museum, Dublin.

LIST OF ILLUSTRATIONS

frontispiece	A view of Trinity Chambers, the firm's office for 100 years, by Muriel Brandt, in 1968.
9	Carlisle (later O'Connell) Bridge in 1873.
26	Bankruptcy and liquidation was long a mainstay of an accountancy practice.
48	The staff in 1883.
55	Three of the partners in 1890.
68,69	The Private Ledger showing the distribution of the great profits of 1898.
79	Dame Street in the early 1900s.
82	Net fees for the three offices 1899-1910.
91	1891-1919 Dublin fees and partners' percentage of fees.
96	The 1907 Exhibition grounds in Herbert Park.
127	1915-1940 Dublin fees and partners' percentage of fees.
146	The Sweep, a cartoon by Heath Robinson.
153	The partners in 1939.
167	The crowds outside Clerys in November 1940.
186	The partners in 1952.
197	1940-1963 Dublin fees and partners' percentage of fees.
211	Partners' length of service 1866-1968.
214	Gardner House in Ballsbridge, Trinity Chambers' successor, by Ruth Brandt.

Introduction

Craig, Gardner and Co.[1] is the longest established accountancy firm in Ireland, having practised continuously under that name since 1866, and having a 'pre-history' that goes back to the Famine years. As Dr Howard Robinson's *A History of Accountants in Ireland* relates, the firm quickly became the leading accountancy practice in the country and, following the amalgamations and mergers that changed the face of the profession in the 1970s, very clearly remained one. Craig Gardner partners took a leading part in the development of accountancy in Ireland, with no fewer than seven of them serving as Presidents of the Institute since the granting of the Charter in 1888, including the very first President, Sir Robert Gardner.

The scope of this history runs up to 1968, the year Craig Gardners moved from the offices it had occupied for just over one hundred years to what turned out to be relatively temporary quarters in Ballsbridge. By this time the firm had recognisably taken on its present internal structure. Externally, the relationship with the international firm of Price Waterhouse was well under way, and would soon be followed by amalgamations with firms in Cork and Limerick. The profession was about to face new problems relating to accounting standards, the growth and complexity of tax legislation and the influence of computers. It is yet too early to take a proper perspective on the long-term effects of these challenges.

This history attempts to show how an individual firm developed and grew inside the framework of the history of accountancy in Ireland. The pressures on the partners and staff from changing commercial and industrial environments, from the social problems of a long political

---

[1] The comma was dropped in the 1940s on the suggestion of the solicitor Arthur Cox.

revolution, and even from advancing age or a preference for other activities, affected the way in which they approached their professional tasks. Generations of men and women built up the firm: an important part of the history is to describe as far as possible how it was organised as a place of work.

In the course of the hundred years or so covered by this book Craig Gardner became deeply embedded in the commercial and industrial life of Ireland. By 1882 the firm had clients in sixty towns and villages throughout Ireland. Since the turn of the century Craig Gardner have been auditors and advisors to a third of the companies quoted on the Dublin Stock Exchange. Decade after decade the firm's activities on behalf of its clients provide vivid cameos of Irish social and business history: the incorporation of the drapery store McBirney's in 1874, the setting up of the great bakery of Johnston, Mooney and O'Brien in 1889, the liquidation of the *Freeman's Journal*, the Sweep, the flotation of P.J. Carrolls, the audit of the new state transport company Córas Iompair Éireann (CIE), and Shanahan's stamp auction liquidation, to name only some of the best-known events in the period covered by this book.

As prominent men in the commercial life of Dublin, the firm's senior people also became involved in activities outside the profession: for example between 1902 and 1908 Sir Robert Gardner rescued the finances of the Pembroke urban council; David Telford was for many years Chairman of the Gaiety Theatre and the Theatre Royal; in 1949 Gabriel Brock retired from the firm to become fulltime Chairman of the Provincial Bank; the previous year Eustace Shott had written a long memo to the government suggesting the establishment of what eventually became the Industrial Development Authority; Gerard O'Brien was lecturer and later Professor of Accountancy at University College, Dublin, from 1935 to 1971.

Accountants are by nature practical rather than philosophical people, and are not inclined to view their working papers and day-to-day documents as sources of history.

INTRODUCTION

As a result the materials for this history have not been abundant. Workbooks survive for 1872-75 and for 1883-86, listing clients, sometimes fees, and occasionally identifying the work done. The firm's private ledgers from 1890 to 1968 survive, giving an unbroken sequence of earnings and expenditure. Partnership deeds going back to 1875 have supplied basic information. Various other documents have also survived which provide contemporary insights, such as John Mackie's long memo of 1924 detailing the new office arrangements, and the minutes of the series of partners' meetings between 1957 and 1964 that radically reset the structure of the firm.

Apart from these documents, the history is based on Gerard O'Brien's typescript *Notes for the History of Craig Gardner*, which was the source of the project; O'Brien, who joined the firm in 1927, also supervised the progress of the writing from the beginning, and provided many insights during several interviews. Many other Craig Gardner sources provided information, and a list of those who helped is given in the acknowledgements.

Other sources of information are cited where they are first used in a chapter but, to reduce the number of notes, not always thereafter. Two books on the history of accountancy deserve special mention as providing in different ways the background against which this story is written: Dr Howard Robinson's *A History of Accountants in Ireland* 2nd edn (Dublin 1983) and Edgar Jones' *Accountancy and the British Economy 1840-1980* (London 1981).

CHAPTER 1

THE VERY BEGINNING

In the 1860s the accountancy profession was still very small — a mere 27 individuals — and two firms were listed in *Thom's Directory* in 1866. Like many other such groups, it was still in the process of defining its exact territory (a few years before one of the accountants listed in *Thom's Directory* had recorded that he also specialised in translating French and German documents !). Many people saw accountants as a specialised adjunct of the legal profession, particularly in respect to bankruptcy work, as was clearly their role in Scotland, and for years, as lawyers and accountants sorted out what was each others' proper business, 'boundary disputes' disfigured relations between the two professions. The problem flared up again when company incorporation had become a relatively routine business. But nonlegal work such as land agency had long been a source of business, as had agencies for insurance companies, debt collection and so on. Accountancy was, however, clearly part of the financial sector: serving the more sophisticated needs of the monetary economy, in the growth of which it therefore had a direct interest.

Much of the profession's business was in insolvency. At this time the law took the view that bankruptcy as such was only available to traders, who were subject to adverse winds outside their control. Private individual persons were held responsible for every penny, unless they could make an arrangement with their creditors. Non-traders were still subject to imprisonment for debt. Although most people in this situation were allowed bail, more than a hundred debtors a year were held in prison. It was therefore important to identify exactly who could be considered a trader. Section XC of the 1857 Bankruptcy and Insolvency Act[1] covers the point with a long list of qualifying trades, including 'alum makers, apothecaries, auctioneers, bankers, bleachers, brokers, brick makers, builders, calenderers, carpenters, . . .' and so on through the alphabet. Accountants as such were not included, though there was a category of 'persons using the trade or profession of a scrivenor

[1] W. Kisbey *Statutes relating to Bankruptcy and Debtors in Ireland* (Dublin 1873).

receiving other men's money or estates into their trust or custody'.

In the 1860s, when William Graham Craig first took his employee Robert Gardner as his partner, Ireland's population was half a million greater than it is now, but a much greater proportion, over 80 per cent, lived and worked in the country. Dublin was an intimate city, with just over 325,000 people in all, an increasing proportion of whom lived in self-administering, mainly Protestant, suburbs such as Rathmines, Pembroke and Clontarf. The 1861 Census revealed that 70,323 people lived in these Dublin suburbs, and 254,808 inside the canal boundaries.[2]

The chief impetus for the growth of the accountancy profession which occurred throughout Europe in the decades after the 1840s was the development of large-scale joint-stock businesses, particularly railways. By April 1846 the British parliament had authorised 519 railway bills, with authorised capital of £304 million. Of these, 43 schemes were Irish, with an authorised capital of £23 million. The bookkeeping techniques that had been sufficient for relatively small merchant houses, however meticulously carried out, were clearly no longer enough, and the special skills of the accountancy profession grew up to supply the need. New ways had to be evolved to distinguish between ownership and management, and to control and report incomes and expenditures on a newly huge scale. In the process of doing so the profession effectively imposed a common language of ledgers, accounts and most importantly double entry bookkeeping on a wide range of commercial and non-commercial activities.

Business from limited liability companies was not prominent in Ireland. A directory published in 1901 noted that there were only 34 limited liability companies registered in Ireland in 1864, most of these being town lighting schemes,

---

[2] M. Daly *Dublin — the Deposed Capital* (Cork 1984).

Carlisle (later O'Connell) Bridge in 1873 – the horse-drawn tram service to south Dublin was started a year before, and in 1875 several companies combined to become the Dublin United Tramway Co., a Craig Gardner client until it in turn amalgamated into CIE.

finance companies and linen concerns.[3] The limited liability concept was still regarded with suspicion by the more conservative commercial element. The other modern mainstays, tax and management consultancy, would not surface as important sources of business for many years. Income tax, which had only been extended to Ireland ten years before, was 4d in the pound, and Gladstone had still not abandoned his long-held ambition of abolishing it altogether. Not that the payers were any more enthusiastic about paying than they are now: a leading London accountant told a Select Committee in the 1860s that he did not believe a suggested technical reform would increase the correctness of returns. His own clients, of course, made correct returns, but the 'lower order of traders' did not. 'I am very afraid, their morality would not be much increased [by the suggested reform] . . . many of them have no consciences at all.'[4]

The history of Craig Gardner & Co., however, stretches further back. In 1858 Henry Brown, an accountant in Dublin, took William Graham Craig as his partner. Brown was a vigorous and enterprising man, the son of a jeweller and silversmith, born in 1817. He had matriculated in Trinity in 1836, but left two years later without a degree, on his father's sudden death. After some years in general commercial life, Brown advertised his services as a 'public accountant' in the *Dublin Almanac* of 1845, announcing that he 'begs to apprise his friends and the public that he is prepared to receive any orders in his line. H.B. can produce vouchers from parties by whom he has been employed,

---

[3] Michael Crowley *Directory and Statistics of Limited Liability Companies registered in Ireland* (Dublin 1901).
[4] B.E.V. Sabine *A History of Income Tax* (London 1966) p 86. The accountant was J.E. Coleman, senior partner in Coleman, Turquand, Young, the first accountant to be appointed auditor to a railway company, and one of the City of London's leading liquidators.

testifying entire satisfaction for accuracy, etc.' He had offices at 2, Fownes Street (where his mother kept the jewellery business going) and at 72, Blessington Street. Exactly what his 'line' might be is suggested by a rival of Brown's, William Hayes, also 'Public Accountant', who described his service thus in the *Dublin Almanac* of 1844: 'Nobody but a person who filled the department of Accountant in a mercantile house, as the advertiser did for a period of twenty years, is qualified to balance accounts involving the slightest complexity . . . those therefore who are preparing to account, whether to Partners or principals, or to Courts, or who wish to have their Books on such a principle as will enable them to do so at any period . . . will find it their interest to apply'.

The Ireland of 1845 was not the most promising place or time to start an accountancy practice. The economy was still suffering from the re-opening of the world food market after the Napoleonic wars: agricultural prices had not recovered to their 1815 levels. Over large tracts there was little trade to speak of, except what was based on barter and local exchange, and so there was very little demand for the services of accountants. On the other hand there was to be, over the next forty years, a rapid expansion of the money economy, and of business practice and cast of mind. The volume of deposits and cash balances increased ten-fold between 1840 and 1914, and the number of bank branches and sub-branches was to rise nearly five-fold to over 800 in the same period.[5]

The country was about to suffer a great national disaster — the Famine. The impact was felt particularly in the poorer areas of the south and west, and huge numbers either died or took the boats to Britain and America. The experience of the Famine in middle-class Dublin, however,

---

[5] O. MacDonagh 'The Victorian Bank, 1824-1914' in F.S.L. Lyons (ed.) *Bicentenary Essays, Bank of Ireland 1783-1983* (Dublin 1983) p 49.

was muted. In fact the population of the city increased 13 per cent during the period. For accountants, at least, the commercial crisis which began in London in 1847 would have been more significant. This was the most severe panic since 1825, and was caused by a combination of the failure of the potato crop, the rapid rise and then collapse of grain prices, falls in railway shares and the French revolution in 1848. Over 500 merchants went bankrupt during this time, including several large Irish houses. Several banks suffered more or less severe runs, and the London and Dublin Bank, with branches in Dublin, Dundalk, Birr, Kells, Mullingar and Wicklow was forced to close its doors.[6]

In the country, more and more estates got into difficulties through the inability of tenants to pay rent, combined with crippling increases in Poor Law rates levied in an attempt to alleviate the crisis. For many landed families the only solution was to sell their estates through the Encumbered Estates Court, which was created in 1849 to simplify the procedures for the sale of bankrupt estates. This court enabled families to break the legal logjam which for generations had made the sale of estates, if not impossible, at least extremely expensive. In the years after the Famine the logjam broke, and more than a quarter of Ireland's land changed hands through this court. Over 95 per cent of the purchasers were Irish, mainly younger sons of gentry, solicitors and shopkeepers who had done well out of the Famine. One long-term effect was to divert absentee rents from England to Dublin. These events also represented a source of new business for accountants and solicitors, as the land market generally opened up, and the new purchasers took stock of their possessions.

---

[6] This account of the 1847/8 crisis is based on F. Hall *The Bank of Ireland 1783-1946* (Dublin 1949) pp 216-221, and D. Morier Evans *The Commercial Crisis 1847-48* (London 1849) passim.

The Very Beginning

By 1858 Brown was so busy that he took on a partner, a move he announced in *Thom*'s with customary verve:

> Audit Office. Henry Brown, Accountant, 2, College Green, offices of the Norwich Union Assurance Company, and late of 2 Fownes' Street begs to announce to his numerous kind Friends and Patrons that, owing to his increasing business, he has this day concluded arrangements with Mr W.G. Craig, late of the Bank of Ireland, to carry on this office in Partnership, under the title of
> BROWN, CRAIG and Company,
> Agents and Accountants.
> H.B. holds the highest testimonials from Noblemen in this country, and Merchants of the first standing, both in Dublin and Belfast, expressive of their appreciation of his abilities as Auditor of Agents' Accounts, Agent for Winding up Estates, and Professional Accountant.
>
> H.B. selects one of each class, received lately by him. First from Sir James Stewart, Bart.
>
> Dear Mr Brown, — Now that you have brought to so happy an issue the Accounts between my land agents and myself, of upwards of thirty years standing, and have turned a large balance claimed by them into one of equal amount in my favour, I cannot deny myself the pleasure of expressing to you the high sense I entertain of the great ability, clearness and sound judgement you displayed in clearing up and rendering intelligible accounts, which from the manner in which they have been kept and the long period for which they had remained unsettled renders the task one of great difficulty, and requiring first-class ability. I may fairly say that it is owing to your ability and patient labour that I have been saved a Chancery suit, which could not have terminated more satisfactorily as to the accounts themselves, and would have been attended with tenfold the expense. In future, should such lie in

your way of business, I should like annually to send you my Agent's accounts to audit.
8th August 1858

From Alexander Parker, Esq., on conclusion of 'Winding up an Estate' satisfactorily, without resorting to bankruptcy:-
'I have been concerned with matters which Mr Brown has undertaken to settle, where accounts have been involved, and many difficulties have beset a proper adjustment; and I have admired the ability, address and perseverance he has displayed in working out a satisfactory conclusion.'

From J.W. McMaster of firm of Dunbar, McMaster & Company, Belfast.

Dear Sir, — I have pleasure in bearing testimony to the high satisfactory manner in which you investigated and squared up the troublesome and intricate accounts over which I had the supervision. My communication with you then has led me to form the opinion that you are a very clever, painstaking Acct. and a hard-working, straighforward man.
August 30th, 1858
H.B. has been appointed by the Court of Chancery Receiver for an Estate at present; and the firm will undertake Land and Estate Agency, at the usual percentage and with security for intromissions.
B.C. and Co. have fitted up a Board-Room at 2, College Green for 'Meetings of Creditors'. Debtors desirous of consulting with their creditors are recommended to communicate with this office, from which summonses are issued, and thus avoid any unnecessary publicity by holding a meeting at their own place of business.
October 1, 1858

Unfortunately nothing is known in detail of work that Brown and Craig undertook, but it is clear that in spite of the general address 'Audit Office', actual auditing as it is now understood was probably a very minor part of their business. Indeed Sir James Stewart seems to be in some doubt as to whether, as he puts it, 'such [would] lie in your way of business'. The patronising tone of the second and third testimonials suggest that they were prompted by Brown for the sake of the advertisement. They make it clear, however, that what the clients valued was a persevering, painstaking ability to sort out other people's financial messes.

This part of the accountants' work was to remain prominent until the 1960s; it amounted to the steady application of the technology of double entry bookkeeping to more or less incomplete records. It is clear from surviving records that the best practice in commercial houses and estates was based on the manuals of bookkeeping that had been published in Ireland since the 1720s, and which were widely used in education, particularly in Quaker schools and other dissenting academies. Most of these manuals, though not all, would have recommended the use of double entry bookkeeping. However even in the best cases, the actual systems in use would often fail to distinguish between capital and current costs, between household and business expenditure and so on.

With the creation of the railway network in the 1850s and 1860s, and the increasing integration of the British and Irish economies, Dublin's importance as a trading centre grew rapidly for twenty years. In 1860 inward and outward tonnage through Dublin port reached one million tons for the first time; two million was reached in 1878, by which time Dublin was the fifth largest port in the British Isles. The increase in imported goods was, however, bad for local manufacturing, and there was a steady decline in industrial employment throughout the second half of the century. The surviving companies specialised in beer, whiskey and biscuits, and in Belfast shipbuilding and linen thrived. Cattle, sheep, pigs and porter constituted the major exports: imports of coal, flour and wheat were prominent.

Because of the slow development of the industrial sector, the skills of the accountancy profession were deployed in different areas. The large estates were usually managed by agents for landlords resident in Dublin or London. Since the agents were chosen more for their gentlemanly qualities than their competence, the scope for muddle was wide. It was obviously only a short step from sorting out agents' accounts to acting as land agents themselves. Agency work was particularly important for Brown, Craig and Co. Not only did they describe themselves in advertisments as 'Agents and Accountants', in that order, but in 1866 they were the only accountants who were still listed under both of these classifications in *Thom's Directory*. Seven years before, a quarter of the accountants had listed themselves also as agents.

Craig's early employment in the Bank of Ireland gives us a few clues as to his otherwise obscure background. Since the Bank employed only some four hundred men at this time, and employment there was eagerly sought, his family must have had some point of contact with the Bank. As one of the Directors explained to an Enquiry in 1873, the bank clerks were generally 'merchants' sons, sons of gentlemen and clergymen and some few shopkeepers' sons.' The Bank was strongly Protestant, and predominantly Church of Ireland. Since salaries were very small in the early years of probation, the need for a protracted period of family support implies a degree of 'gentlemanliness'. On the other hand the Bank was not competing very successfully with its newer commercial rivals. Its share of total private bank deposits fell from 34 per cent in 1845 to 12 per cent in 1864. Much of the failure of the Bank to progress was attributed, at least by the Directors, to a legal prohibition against lending money on land mortgages. In the busy land market of the 1850s, this was felt to be a major handicap, though the commercial success of the Bank did not noticeably improve when the limitation was removed by statute in

1860. It is easy to envisage that Craig may not have been too difficult to entice away from the low pay, commercial weakness and authoritarian atmosphere of the Bank.[7]

Two years later, Brown, Craig and Co. issued an advertisement which reflects the early days of the corporate sector as an important field of activity for accountants, even if through the familiar insolvency route. They now describe themselves as Auditors and Public Accountants rather than Agents and Accountants.

> Brown, Craig and Co., Auditors and Public Accountants, 2 College Green (Head Office), Agents for Winding up estates, secretaries for public companies, official liquidators and general agents, B.C. & Co having increased demands on them, have opened Extra Offices at No. 4 College Green, (Branch Office) whereby they hope to meet every call upon them.
> In the Court of Chancery, Master Brooke, on the appointment of H. Brown as 'Official Liquidator' in the matter of the Joint Stock Companies Winding-up Act 1848-9, and of the Dublin Gas Independent Consumer's Company, stated:-
> As he had received the highest testimonials in favour of Mr Brown, both public and private, which reflected great credit upon him, he approved of the nomination. Attached to the offices is a Board Room at 2 College Green for meetings of Directors of Public Companies, and for Creditors Meetings in winding-up estates. H.B. is at present acting as Liquidator for the Royal Irish Fisheries Company.

---

[7] O. MacDonagh 'The Victorian Bank, 1824-1914' in F.S.L. Lyons (ed.) *Bicentenary Essays, Bank of Ireland 1783-1983* (Dublin 1983). In 1857 the Court of Directors announced that matchboxes were henceforth outlawed from the clerks' desks — anyone disobeying would 'incur their displeasure'.

The following gratifying testimony was lately received from the respectable firm of Messrs. Francis Ritchie and Sons, Belfast:-
We have carefully examined the accounts and statements of the affairs of Mr. —— , in connexion with his ... contract, and are fully satisfied with their accuracy, and believing that the estate is only capable of paying a dividend of ... shillings in the pound, have accepted same. We, as well as other creditors, have much cause to be obliged to Mr Brown for his valuable assistance in obtaining so favourable a settlement.
Francis Ritchie & Sons
Merchants, Traders and others, protected from risk and fraud.
Accounts collected upon a simple and efficient system.
November 1859

Bankruptcies and liquidations are obviously important, but now the Board Room is for Directors' as well as creditors' meetings, and the beginnings of the Secretarial department can be seen. Debt collecting is still done, and it was to remain a service offered for more than twenty years.

In 1865 Brown, Craig and Co. moved from College Green to Trinity Chambers, 40/41 Dame Street, Dublin. The firm was to stay in these premises for just over one hundred years, until pressure on space forced it to move to Ballsbridge in 1968. The new office had just been completed at the end of 1864, and was designed by the Scottish architect David Bruce for the Life Association of Scotland Assurance Company. A British trade magazine, *The Builder*, described the building in its issue of 3 December 1864:

The extensive and costly pile of buildings styled the Life Association of Scotland Chambers having just been completed, the office opened for business a few days ago. The site selected for the structure is perhaps the most central in the city of Dublin, presenting a frontage of 41 ft in Dame-street, opposite the Chamber of Commerce, and returning 43 ft in Trinity-street adjoining. No expense has been spared to render this building a creditable representation of the magnificent offices erected for the company in Edinburgh, founded in 1838. The entire of each facade, five stories in height, being faced with dressed ashlar masonry from the Kenmure quarries.[8]

The Italian style of architecture, of Palladian character, has been adopted. The ground floor, presenting a series of rusticated piers, extends to the top of the entresol storey, having moulded joints and vermiculated faces, surmounted by a frieze and cornice. The windows in the upper stories are ornamented with balconies and balusters, moulded architraves, carved consoles, and alternate, straight, and segmental pediments. A deep frieze, enriched with metopes and modillions, and high balustrade, conceals the windows which light the apartments in the roof. The office entrance, situate in the centre of the principal front, is decorated with pilasters supporting projecting consoles and rusticated arch, with enriched keystone and pediment. The doors are of Riga oak, panelled, moulded, and varnished.

The ground floor affords accommodation for the business of the company, consisting of public offices, secretary's room, fireproof safe, board-room, doctor's-room, retiring-room, etc.; having a commodious set of offices for letting on the right of central entrance, with basement storey for each suite of offices, lighted by windows above the level of street paving.

---

[8] Much later these facings began to fall off, to the peril of passers-by, and so had to be expensively replaced.

The works have been executed by Messrs. Morrison, under the direction of the consulting architect, Mr. Bryce, of Edinburgh; and superintending architect, Mr. Charles Geoghegan, of Dublin. The total outlay on the premises has been about £8,000. The execution of the office counters, desks, framings, and furniture is well calculated to sustain the reputation of the manufacturer, Mr William Brunton.

The announcement of Brown, Craig's move in the *Thom*'s of that year was less spirited than previous announcements, perhaps reflecting Craig's more sober approach, since subsequent advertisements, which were certainly drafted by Brown, revert to his grandiloquent style.

Audit Office, Trinity Chambers, 40 and 41 Dame Street, Dublin. Brown, Craig and Co., Public Accountants are engaged in all matters of account in Chancery, Bankruptcy, Partnership Accounts, Rentals, etc. also in opening Books of Public Companies, in accordance with the provisions of the Joint-Stock Companies' Act, winding-up Estates as Liquidators, acting as Auditors, and as Scrutators in all questions of dispute and reference
Agents of the Royal Insurance Company.

In May 1866 the great City of London bill-broking firm of Overend, Gurney suspended payment, with liabilities of over £10m. The scale of this crash is indicated by the fact that at this time the total value of all bank notes in circulation from the Irish banks was less than £6m, and the reserves of the Bank of England were only £20m. At once a 'panic' ensued, the worst for twenty years. It particularly hit a sector of highly speculative finance companies that had sprung up to promote limited liability ventures. Several of these had financed Irish projects, particularly in railway development and shipping.

When the crisis broke many of these companies were ruined, taking with them 'a considerable number of Irish shareholders'.[9]

Henry Brown went on business to London at this time, very likely in connection with the aftermath of the crisis. In his absence, William Craig had to look round for another partner, and soon found one in the person of Robert Gardner, who probably worked in the office. The new partnership started trading under the name of Craig, Gardner & Company in 1866.

A year later Brown returned to Dublin and set up by himself. In 1868 he took a partner and the firm was renamed Brown, Reid and Company. One of his clients was the Dublin Zoo, whose accounts his firm prepared in 1883-5; although Gardner was an enthusiastic member of the Zoo from 1881 to 1919, the audit did not come to Craig Gardner until 1985, one hundred years after Brown's last audit. By 1887 Brown was a Justice of the Peace, and was second only to Robert Gardner in the list of signatories to the petition for incorporation of the Institute. At the inaugural dinner of the Institute in 1888, Henry Brown claimed, with some justice, that 'he might be considered the father of the profession in Ireland'. The first President of the Institute, Robert Gardner (an ex-employee of Brown's), expressed the point somewhat differently; he described Brown as 'the oldest accountant in Ireland'. Brown became the second President in 1890, a post he held for four years. He died in 1902.

---

[9] F. Hall *The Bank of Ireland 1783-1946* (Dublin 1949) pp 245-8.

The First Craig Gardner Partnership, 1866-75

The new partner, Robert Gardner, had been born in 1838 in Ballymoney, a town between Ballymena and Coleraine, in County Antrim. He was educated privately in Ballymoney, and had worked in Dublin as an accountant since he was nineteen, joining Brown, Craig and Co. in 1856. Ballymoney was then a town of just over 2,000 inhabitants, with 11,500 in the surrounding countryside. The principal business of the area was linen, and Ballymoney's market was 'eminent for the superior quality of the goods sold'.[10] The town also had an extensive trade in linen and agricultural products with Liverpool and London.

The shape of Craig Gardner's business in those early days can be seen very clearly in the oldest extant record of the firm, a Private Journal running from 1872 to 1877. It is written up in Robert Gardner's flowing, somewhat careless hand (the very first page contains the unorthodox spelling, *leger a/c*, a version that was later to be stamped in leather on the Private Ledger that ran from 1890-1924). The book contains listings of clients and fees for each half year to 1 February and 1 August. At those dates a profit and loss statement for the six-month period is drawn up, showing the details of salaries and other expenses set against the total income. Finally, the distribution of the resulting profits to the partners is calculated.

In the very first half-year (to 1 February 1872) the total fee account amounts to £2143 16s 4d. Expenses were £699 12s 9d, plus £79 9s 5d for bad debts written off and interest on partners' capital.[11] The partners' share was therefore

---

[10] S. Lewis *Topographical Dictionary of Ireland* (Dublin 1837).
[11] Hereafter all sums will be given in round pounds, though they are of course always expressed in full in the ledgers.

64 per cent of fees. Profits were divided into twelfths, with William Craig taking seven twelfths, which gave him £796 for the half-year, and Robert Gardner five twelfths, or £569. Interest was calculated at 5 per cent, which was approximately the rate on an Irish three-month bill. Salaries (to employees, not partners) came to £345, though there is no indication how many men were employed. Rent and furniture for a Belfast office were charged against income, but this item disappears in subsequent accounts (to be replaced by a subscription to the *Belfast Newsletter*), so presumably it was decided not to maintain the office. Craig Gardner's next attempt to set up a Belfast office, in 1894, was more long-lived.

The client list details 114 jobs billed in the six-month period, yielding a gross income of £1788; income from other sources came to £356 (17 per cent). The firm was agent for the Royal Insurance Company, and there is later evidence of speculation in shares. As a sign of things to come, 14 per cent of income comes from limited companies, but there is still a good sprinkling of land accounts for the nobility — Lords Clonmel, Howth and St Lawrence for instance. Over half of the fees are £7 or less. Three fees accounted for 20 per cent of the income, and the average is just less than £16. This compares with one large City of London firm, for which records are extant, which in 1870 had eleven clients with fees of more than £500, and a top fee of £4,277 for a liquidation.[12] The conditions of the Irish economy for many years forced Craig Gardner to rely on a relatively large number of small fees.

In 1872 the Court of Bankruptcy in Ireland laid down a set of standard fees that it would allow for insolvency work:[13]

---

[12] E. Jones *Accountancy and the British Economy* 1840-1980 (London 1981) p 63.
[13] Kisbey *Statutes relating to Bankruptcy and Debtors in Ireland* (Dublin 1873) p 279.

for investigating and preparing accounts, balance sheets, reports etc.,
Principal's time, for each day of eight hours.   £2.2.0
Clerk or assistant's time ditto   10/- to 15/-

The firm's average fee of just under £16 therefore represented possibly three or four days of a principal's time and ten or twelve clerk-days. From the time taken, one can assume that the bulk of the work was bookkeeping and accounts preparation.

In general the mix of clients is not much different to that which a small accountancy firm might have right up to the present day. Two hotels, a seed merchant, a builder and timber merchant, a piano warehouse, two publishers, two charities, some drapers, a few solicitors, the Ringsend Bottle Company and a stockbroker are among those that can be identified. Most of the identifiable clients recur from year to year.

One small railway company, the Bagnalstown and Wexford, was listed for a fee of £16, but was not to last long on the books, for the company was swallowed by the Great Southern in 1876. From 1874 the Rathmines, Rathgar, Roundtown, Rathfarnham & Rathcoole Railway, which had been incorporated in 1864, with a plan to build a railway from Dame Street to Wicklow via Rathmines, appeared for a couple of years, but the idea eventually came to nothing. More promising was the appearance in 1876 of a £40 fee for 'Tramway Co.'. In 1872 a horse-drawn tram service to south Dublin was initiated, and later three tram companies combined into the Dublin United Tramway Co., which was to prove, many years later still, Craig Gardner's wooden horse into the CIE audit.

Other clients include the builders merchants Brooks Thomas, even then a large firm with five addresses in the city, Breslin Hotels, who owned the Royal Marine and the International Hotels in Dun Laoghaire, and the Home Government Association, the precursor of the Home Rule League. Generally the clients are small — no large banks or insurance companies are listed, for instance. In 1874 the solicitor Michael Larkin brought Craig Gardner in as auditors to the drapers McBirney's, who were incorporated in that year.[14] The procedure was clearly not very familiar to these leaders of their respective professions in Ireland, for Larkin's detailed invoice noted that 'several limited companies having been lately started in Dublin and also some drapery concerns in London, copies of the Articles of Association were procured for the purpose of considering same as to this company.'[15] The fees charged by Craig Gardner were 8 guineas for preparing the accounts and the balance sheet, and 'attending meetings of Directors, arranging as to Minutes of the Company, allotment of shares, cheques on bankers etc.' and 15 guineas for audit and 'checking accounts, balances and additions etc. and certifying same.' In general however, in marked contrast to later years, work clearly identified as coming through solicitors is not prominent, nor are the solicitors themselves.

After 1872 major changes in Irish bankruptcy law provided a new opportunity for accountants. Imprisonment for ordinary debt was abolished, as was the difference between traders and others. Henceforth if anyone was unable to pay their debts they could either resolve their situation through the courts, or the creditors could appoint a trustee in bankruptcy who would deal with the affair.

---

[14] The specific reason for incorporation was to protect the firm against the removal of capital after the death of one or other of the two managing partners. According to Crowley *Directory and Statistics of Limited Liability Companies registered in Ireland* (Dublin 1901), half of the Irish firms incorporated before 1901 were of existing businesses.
[15] McBirney Records in the Business Records section of the Public Records Office.

In the Court of Bankruptcy, Ireland,

In the Matter of a Petition for Arrangement by
Christian Wilson of Sledagh

I beg to inform you that, pursuant to the General Order of this Court, a Preliminary Meeting of Creditors to consider the affairs of the Petitioner will be held at the Office, No. *of Craig Gardiner & Co College Green Dublin* on *Wednesday* the 23 day of *July*, 1873, at the hour of 3 o'clock *after* noon, when a statement of the affairs of the said Petitioner will be submitted to the Meeting.

Dated this *19* day of *July* 1873

H. F. Leachman

Solicitor for the Petitioner,

No. *43 Dame Street*

Bankruptcy and liquidation was long a mainstay of an accountancy practice.

The business grew steadily over the next three years. Annual fees for the year ended on 1 August went from £4,950 in 1872 to £7,143 in 1875. The increase in fees was achieved partly by an increase in the number of jobs (from 114 in the six months to February 1872 to 142 listed for the period to February 1875) and partly by an increase in average fees from £16 to £21 per job.

The proportion of small fees, of three guineas or less, had dropped from 21 per cent to 10 per cent. The seasonal pattern was slightly biased to the summer months, with 55 per cent of income coming between February and August. Salaries fluctuated at between 19 and 24 per cent of fee income, and other expenses were low. In 1875 the ledger records payments to 18 clerks, of whom the three senior men, Cunningham, Furniss and O'Harte, earned between £200 and £240 a year each. Cunningham and O'Harte later left the firm to set up on their own, and were among the 13 original Dublin accountants who signed the petition for incorporation of the Institute.

The income of the two partners grew steadily; in 1875 Craig (still the senior partner on 7/12ths) earned £2,000 a year, as much as a judge in the Bankruptcy Court. Awareness of this perhaps added a touch of acid to Judge Miller's remarks on a case which demonstrated the continuing struggle to define the relative roles of solicitors (incorporated in 1854) and accountants (incorporated 1888). The *Irish Law Times*[16] reported the case thus:

> A member of an eminent firm of accountants was sent down to Mayo to investigate a trader's affairs. In pre-

---

[16] 20 May 1876; the reference to the 'eminent firm of accountants' is a reference either to Craig Gardner or the much newer firm of Brown, Reid.

paring his report, the accountant omitted the name of a creditor because the goods he supplied to the arranging trader had been burned. Judge Miller said that this was an assumption of duty entirely outside the province of an accountant inasmuch as it was practically deciding matters of law. He considered that the solicitors engaged in such cases should keep their business in their own hands, and not allow accountants to take such matters on themselves. He found in one case that an accountant had filed a schedule without the intervention of a solicitor at all, and now he found an arrangement practically conducted without a solicitor. If these gentlemen did not keep themselves in their proper province, he would control them by disallowing their expenses.

The Split

1875 was to see the departure of the senior partner in circumstances that have long been shrouded in mystery. The usual account, which is incidentally the best known event in the firm's history, is described by Dr Robinson thus: 'tradition in Craig Gardner is that [Craig] retired from the firm to enter a mental home after instructing an assistant to proceed to Turkey (which was then the sick man of Europe) and to wind it up, stressing to the assistant that he should take great care to include in the inventory of assets all the national flags and other property of the state. Robert Gardner, on hearing of these instructions, is said to have removed his partner.'[17]

Unfortunately this extraordinary story hardly matches the facts. Certainly it is clear that there was a split between

---

[17] H. Robinson *A History of Accountants in Ireland* 2nd edn (Dublin 1983) p 21.

the two partners in March 1875, which resulted in Robert Gardner setting up on his own in early April of that year. Since the half-year accounts to the end of February that year are done on a going-concern basis, the break must have been sudden. It was announced in two advertisements in the *Irish Commercial and Railway Directory* in this way:

> Audit Office, Trinity Chambers, 40 and 41 Dame Street, Dublin. Craig & Co., Public Accountants, are engaged in all matters of Account in Chancery, Bankruptcy, Partnership Accounts, Rentals &. also in opening the Books of Joint-Stock Companies, in accordance with the provisions of the Joint-Stock Companies Act, winding up Estates as Liquidators, acting as Auditors, &c

and

> Mr R. Gardner, late of Craig, Gardner & Co., has removed his offices from Trinity Chambers, to Nos. 46 and 47 Dame Street, Dublin.

Far from removing his partner, both the wording of the advertisements and the surviving workbooks suggest that Gardner removed himself. He practised as Robert Gardner & Co. for six months from Nos 46 and 47 Dame Street, no doubt with some of the old Craig Gardner clerks. The first pages of the new workbook are headed 'RG & Co.', and 'new a/c' and 'old a/c' presumably identifying those clients he took with him. Most of the work however comes from solicitors such as D. & T. Fitzgerald (later to be solicitors to the Institute), Casey and Clay, Scallan and so on. Virtually all the business seems to be in the new liquidation and insolvency field opened up by the 1872 Act.

Work flowed in fairly rapidly; by the end of the first month 40 jobs were recorded, and by September the new firm had completed over 200 assignments. Most of these were quite small, with an average billing of less than £7 (only a third of Craig Gardner's previous level), and some with fees going as low as half a guinea.

Much of this business must have been achieved at the expense of the old firm now called Craig & Co., and by the summer Craig and Gardner came to an agreement which reunited the two firms. This was embodied in a formal deed, which stated that 'William Graham Craig has determined to dissolve the copartnership and to retire therefrom . . .' Thereafter Robert Gardner could carry on the business on his own, under the name of Craig Gardner or any other he chose. In exchange, Gardner was to give Craig, now of Danescourt, Athboy, County Meath, an annuity of £1,000 a year, payable quarterly, and a lump sum of £1,420, being the difference between the assets and liabilities of the partnership. The agreement goes on to state that Craig shall not set up or exercise in Ireland the business previously carried on by the partnership. If during the five years following the agreement, the profits of the business were less than £1,000 for any half-year, Craig was to be paid half the actual profits. Craig was allowed access to the books every half year for the purpose of ascertaining the position. ascertaining the position.

This agreement was duly executed, and the next page in the workbook is headed 'RG as CG & Co.' In subsequent years payment of the annuity is recorded in the private ledger. Six years later, in 1881, a further deed of agreement was signed, whereby Gardner gave Craig a lump sum of £1,750 in exchange for a release of £250 of the annuity. This new deed describes Craig as having 'in himself good right full power and lawful and absolute authority to assign the said annuity'. He used some of the money at least to buy shares in Arnott's (a Craig Gardner client), which he sold eighteen months later.

The deed of 1875 amounted to Craig selling the business to Gardner in exchange for a pension of half what he had been earning in recent years. The turnover of the firm at this time was about £8,000 a year, and was to increase rapidly over the next few years. The total expenses, including salaries and income tax, took about a half of gross fees; from Gardner's point of view therefore, the deal was a good speculation. On his part Craig was able to retire to the country with a handsome pension, after working in the firm for twenty years.

As to the suddenness of the split, there is some evidence that the temperaments of the two partners may not have been compatible. Gardner was an abrasive, impatient man. Even in the self-congratulatory atmosphere of the inaugural banquet of the Institute in 1888 he was described (to laughter) as 'impetuous' and 'despotic' by his friend and relative by marriage the solicitor William Findlater.[18] His writing in the workbooks and the ledgers is flowing, rapid, and not always accurate. Kennedy is spelt Kennady, imbecile, imbacile and so on. Even totting errors occur, and it is clear from 1874 that someone, presumably Craig, is checking every addition in the ledger. In one case, a sum that Gardner has rounded to £160 is carefully noted to be £159.17s.5d. One can imagine how exasperating this must have been for both men. Craig, professionally formed in the cautious traditions of the Bank of Ireland, may also have found unnerving the increasing proportion of income from the relatively speculative 'Other Sources', which had reached 30 per cent of the whole by 1875.

Whether the story of the attempted liquidation of Turkey is based in truth or not, it has long been part of the firm's folklore. If there is some truth behind it, it is certainly a spectacular episode; if untrue, the creation and careful preservation of such a story down the years has its own interest. Did it, for instance, have its unconscious origins in an small incident or dispute expanded over the years by men loyal to Gardner in an attempt to discredit Craig and to establish a kind of legitimate succession, rather as

---

[18] The inaugural dinner is described in detail in *The Accountant* 1 December 1888.

Richard III was discredited by Shakespeare on behalf of his Tudor patrons? There is, incidentally, no record of a public or private asylum in Meath.

The retirement of the senior partner, however effected, did not stop the growth in the firm's fee income: by September 1877, annual fees had reached £10,095. Gardner was now becoming wealthy. Only a year after the split with Craig he had sufficient capital in hand to buy 1,100 Arnott's £4 shares. To celebrate his new position he moved house, to Ashley, Clyde Road, which he bought from the original owner for £3,000, and where he was to live for the rest of his life. This was a step up from 4 Belgrave Square (East) in Rathmines, his previous address.

The Pembroke township was strongly under the control of the Earl of Pembroke, and unlike Rathmines, did not encourage development. Building permissions were hedged around with stringent clauses on materials and finish, so the township never attracted the volume of speculative building for clerical residents found in Rathmines.[19] As a result it was a much grander place to live: 'large numbers of professional people and many others of good birth and breeding occupied houses in "The Roads". Clyde Road, Elgin Road, Morehampton Road, Pembroke Road, all held good substantial houses, the owners of which were judges, colonels, leading lawyers and country gentry whose places were to let; and many other folk of similar stratum. A pleasant enough society, whose common meeting-ground was the Castle, and the great Dublin houses, and the leading clubs of the time'.[20]

Unfortunately neither the prestige of the area nor the Earl's concern with appearances prevented the drains from being a problem. Despite the expense and size of these houses, sanitary conditions left much to be desired: in the

---

[19] M. Daly *Dublin — the Deposed Capital* (Cork 1984) p 161.
[20] P.L. Dickinson *The Dublin of Yesterday* (London 1929) p 191.

late 1870s an outbreak of typhoid in Raglan Road, Clyde Road and Elgin Road led to deputations to the authorities from concerned householders. During this outbreak, in 1878, Gardner's wife, Sarah Dale, died, leaving him a widower with two sons and two daughters, including John, aged 14, who later became a partner in the firm. Two years later, in January 1880, Gardner remarried, this time to Jane, daughter of his neighbour John Brown Johnston, who owned a number of bakery shops around the city. The Johnstons were connected by marriage to the Findlaters, particularly to John Findlater, who was among other things Chairman of Alex Findlater's, a chain of grocery and wine stores, and first cousin to the solicitor William Findlater, who was both client and a source of business for Craig Gardner. The marriage settlement on Jane included such sophisticated international investments as Russian bonds (£1,000), New York Central Railway bonds ($9,000 worth), and £1,650 Mexican Railway Company shares, but no holdings in any Irish companies.

The end of the 1870s left the firm in the control of Robert Gardner, who at 40 was the sole owner of the biggest accountancy practice in Ireland, a position he was to retain until 1917. During a period when a skilled craftsman was glad to get £100 a year, Gardner was to enjoy an average after-tax income of £3,000 a year for the next forty years. During the years that Robert Gardner was senior partner in the firm, the nature of accounting work and of the accountancy profession changed beyond recognition. A workbook from 1885 shows that only 21 per cent of identified jobs are described as auditing; by far the largest number of these (44 per cent) are concerned with bankruptcy and insolvency. By 1920, when Gardner died, auditing (which included making up accounts and as necessary tax returns) had become the main-spring of the firm. Professionally the accountants of 1920 had been an established chartered body for over thirty years, with a clearly understood set of functions. In the 1870s, they were still struggling to define the difference between their role and that of the solicitors.

CHAPTER 2

SOLE PRACTITIONER 1875-90

The late 1870s and the early 1880s were hard years for the Irish people. Bad harvests in three years running from 1877, in a country dependent on agriculture, led to a major economic crisis in 1879. As a result of poor potato and grain harvests, pig numbers dropped, as did those of cows and sheep. Butter prices fell 50 per cent between 1879 and 1880. Evictions began to rise, and with them rural violence. In 1880 the RIC were armed with buckshot for the first time. Two years later the Chief Secretary and an under-secretary were assassinated in the Phoenix Park. It was the strenuous, highly-charged era of Parnell, Davitt and Captain Boycott. The activities of the Land League on behalf of the tenant farmers in these years were to have a deep and long-lasting effect, freeing them from a psychological dependency on the landlords in a way that served as the essential preliminary of the struggle for independence over the next forty years.

In the country as a whole, people were slow to risk capital in the hazardous enterprise of creating a new industry in such an unpromising economy, and one moreover that was, in a free trade era, constantly exposed to the rivalry of more developed industries across the water. 'A good deal of such capital as existed was either invested out of Ireland altogether or, as frequently happened, was diverted from business use by the Irishman's obsessive pursuit of status, measured either by the acquisition of land or by the education of his children to seek their fulfilment in a profession rather than in trade.'[1] Given the potential earnings in the professions, as exemplified by Gardner's earnings, and by those doctors and lawyers for whom the great houses in south Dublin in the late nineteenth century were built, compared with the extremely uncertain future in industry, the preference for the professional life, as well as being socially attractive, was a perfectly rational economic decision.

---

[1] F.S.L. Lyons *Ireland since the Famine* (London 1973) p 55.

The political troubles, added to Ireland's position on the periphery of the British Isles' economy, and the relative strength of the English industrial and financial markets affected the speed at which the accountancy profession in Dublin could grow. In the City of London Deloittes, which was only one of the leading firms, had been grossing £7,600 in fees in 1874, as opposed to Craig Gardner's £6,762; by 1887 Deloitte's had gross fees of £25,814, as opposed to Craig Gardner's 1890-95 average of £11,800. As a result of this strength, and the spread of English investment money into areas such as the North America, Latin America, Russia and the Far East, British accountancy firms were in a position to take audit and other accountancy work from local accountants in these areas and to establish international practices.

Dublin's growth as a port began, in the 1880s, to be overtaken by Belfast, but the city was still the effective centre of the Irish railway system, which had by now reached 2,500 miles of track. The railway, by presenting a quick and cheap mode of travel, enabled Craig Gardner staff to work on jobs throughout the country. In a work book covering 1881/2 some sixty destinations thoughout Ireland are listed as sources of work. Obvious places such as Belfast, Cork, Dundalk, Galway, Londonderry, Sligo and Waterford are frequently represented, but so are Athlone, Bantry, Balbriggan, Cavan, Cahir, Drogheda, Fermoy, Killorglin, Kilrush, Lismore, Lurgan, Nenagh, Omagh, Roscrea, Swinford, Tralee and Wexford.

Not all of these would have involved travel, though presumably the integration of the country meant that work was at least coming to Craig Gardner which would not have done so before. The tradition of the annual visit of 'the auditor' to the country town began in these years, and with it a new set of problems for the firm. As a visitor from the city, and one moreover entrusted with secrets, the firm's clerks were frequently exposed to lavish hospitality and its attendant risks. William Cunningham recalled travelling by train many years later from Belfast with George Hill

Tulloch, then senior partner. Tulloch looked out of the window as the train passed through Dundalk.

'Gloomy place, Dundalk,' he said. 'We lost a lot of good men there. They had nothing to do in the evening and took to drink.'

The Nature of the Work in the 1880s

By 1883 over 20,000 limited companies had been registered in the British Isles. But 'many limited companies were dissolved almost as fast as they were formed. In the second half of the nineteenth century about one-quarter of companies were dissolved within three years of registration, about one-half within ten years and getting on for three-quarters within twenty years.'[2] The looseness of the law allowed 'bubble' companies to be easily founded, which just as quickly collapsed through fraud or gross mismanagement. The rate of dissolution of limited liability companies was somewhat lower in Ireland, but still considerable. The 1862 Companies Act had no clauses requiring the Directors to present statements of account to the shareholders, nor did it require an audit.

Even when auditors were appointed (and the model form of memorandum printed as a Schedule to the Act certainly proposed that they should be) they were nearly always shareholders and not professional men. A Scots accountant summed up the situation in Hong Kong a few years later: 'if a gentleman — a good fellow, of course — was not too successful in business, then pickings would be found for him

---

[2] J. Kitchen and R.H. Parker *Accounting Thought and Education — Six English Pioneers* (London 1980) p 30 — the information that follows on Edwin Guthrie and F.W. Pixley is also based on this source.

by giving him auditor's fees here and there'.[3] This reflected a considerable scepticism among business people as to the usefulness of an audit. As *Herapath's Railway Journal* asked in 1878, 'what is the use of an audit? When did it ever bring to light a state of things which was radically and seriously wrong?' The magazine described the work of Quilter Ball, a leading British firm: 'the audit they perform [of a railway company] is perfectly useless — the time occupied in such an enquiry being limited to one or two visits in the half-year and those only of a few hours each'.

As late as 1900, the Great Northern Railway, with an annual turnover of £895,000, employed two non-professional auditors, who were paid £50 a year each. In 1910 the Great Southern and Western Railway transported over six million passengers and had a turnover of £1.5 million, and still employed non-professional auditors. In fact these two companies, by far the largest on the Irish railway system, did not have their accounts signed by professional accountants until 1913, when the Railway Companies (Accounts and Returns) Act, 1911, came into effect. They then both chose English firms, the Great Northern's accounts being 'examined and approved' by Deloitte Plender Griffith and the Great Southern and Western by Price Waterhouse.

Bankers were no keener on auditors than businessmen. The *Bankers' Magazine* of January 1887 wrote: 'Bankers are now busy balancing their books for 1886 ... in the midst of this heavy work they are interrupted by what becomes a perfect nuisance, the interference of the professional auditor and his clerks ... With all their ability, their ignorance of banking practice continually finds them wanting, and they pass over, year after year, the very cobwebs they are supposed to discover.'[4]

---

[3] J. Graham *The Lowe Bingham Story* (Hong Kong 1977) p 11.
[4] Quoted in N. Simpson *The Belfast Bank 1827-1970* (Belfast 1975) pp 153-4.

Clearly the theory and practice of auditing in the 1880s had some way to go; in fact the first book on the subject, F.W. Pixley's *Auditors: Their Duties and Responsibilities*, was only published in 1881. In other respects too, accountancy practice was quite unformed. In 1882 the Manchester accountant Edwin Guthrie published an article about the presentation of accounts,[5] in which he discusses whether assets or liabilities should fall on the right-hand side of the Balance Sheet, what the difference is between an income and expenditure account and a receipts and payments statement, and recommends that stock be shown as part of the cost of goods sold or manufactured. The article aroused great interest, and stimulated many letters. The Irish profession, however, with a few exceptions, was not given to theorising. When Robert Gardner sponsored a prize in 1888 for an essay on auditing, only four entries were received, despite the handsome endowment. The winner, F.J. McGovern, was employed by Craig Gardner (W.H. Knight of Atkins of Cork[6] came second). Craig Gardner themselves prepared the accounts of Arnott's with the capital and liabilities on the right-hand side until 1896.

A further indication of the relative underdevelopment of the auditing side is the wording of the auditor's report printed on the accounts sent to shareholders. The firm's normal form by the end of the century, as used for instance on the Convoy Woollen Company's accounts in 1889, was: 'We have examined the foregoing Accounts, compared same with the Books of the Company, and found same correct. In our opinion the Balance Sheet is properly drawn up and discloses the true state of the Company's affairs.' The formula wasn't rigid as it later became; one variant

[5] 'The Want of Uniformity in Accounts' *The Accountant* 28 October 1882.
[6] Later Atkins, Chirnside, which amalgamated with Craig Gardner in the 1970s.

ran: 'We have examined the foregoing balance sheet and profit and loss account and have compared the same with the Books and found them to agree. In our opinion the Balance Sheet discloses the true state of the Company's affairs as shown by the said Books.' Occasionally, however, the firm used a laconic and dangerously comprehensive form, simply: 'Audited and found Correct'.

Pixley, in his *Chartered Accountants' Charges*,[7] describes the progress of a typical audit job of the time, in the form of a standard invoice.

> For time occupied by Principals and clerks attending you and receiving your instructions to audit the Accounts of your Firm for the year ending 31st December 18..
> Perusing Deed of Partnership, dated 18.. and making notes therefrom.
>
> Attending at your Offices and engaged with your Bookkeeper, Mr ——, when he handed us a list of the books in use and he informed us that he was unable to balance the books.
> Accordingly reporting this to you when you instructed us to balance the books.
> Calling over the postings from the Day Books, Invoice Books and Cash Book, into the Ledgers, when we discovered a great number of errors.
> Checking and correcting where necessary the additions of the Day Books and Invoice Books.
> On ascertaining that the Private Ledger and Impersonal Ledger were imperfectly kept, making the necessary entries and correcting entries.
> Balancing the books and taking out Trial Balance.

---

[7] (London 1889) pp 17-19. This book was among a number donated to the library of the Irish Institute by Pixley.

Raising therefrom Trading and Profit and Loss account for the year ending 31st December 18.. also Balance Sheet or Statement showing the financial position of the Firm at that date.
Drafting report showing the result of our audit, and the errors in the method of book-keeping and fair copying same.
Fair copying Profit and Loss Account, Balance Sheet, and the Capital and Drawing Accounts of the Partners into books specially prepared for that purpose in accordance with the Articles of Partnership.
Correspondence, etc.

Time Occupied	£	s	d
Principals, 35 hours = 5 days at £5 5s	26	5	0
1st class clerks, 94 hours = 13 3/7 days at £1 11s 6d	21	3	0
Other clerks, 273 hours = 39 days at £1 1s	40	19	0
	88	7	0
Disbursements, stationery, etc.	1	4	6
	89	11	6

This related to a London practice, and no doubt some Craig Gardner jobs were just like that. Much of the work of an Irish accountancy practice at this time however was still related to frauds and failures: arranging debtors (A/D), liquidations, bankruptcies, investigations, selling off stock and trust accounts were all still important. Debt collecting, which was discouraged by the English Institute, appears to have been dropped by 1887. The mix of jobs taken in January 1884 is typical (see Table 1 below).

Few of these jobs recurred from year to year, so the firm was dependent on a constant flow of new business. This gave rise to substantial year-to-year fluctuations in

Table 1: Workload in January 1884

Type of job	No.
Audit	15
Bankruptcy, Liquidation, A/D	23
Trust estates, decd.	4
Others*	9
Not described[8]	39
Total	90

*including fire claim, debt collection, half-year accounts, opening books, stocktaking, security valuation, etc.

income, a feature of Craig Gardner's earnings that was not to change until after 1900, when a more steady pattern set in. For instance, fees were charged on 584 jobs in 1883/4, but on only 421 in 1885/6.

The firm, and particularly Robert Gardner himself, had at this time a dominant position in the accountancy world, particularly in insolvency work. In 1883 the national total of bankruptcies, liquidations and arrangements was 911:[9] from the workbooks, Craig Gardner's seem to have been involved in a quarter of all of these, and probably a larger proportion of those with substantial assets. The drastic fall in business between 1883 and 1885 no doubt reflects the decline in the wave of insolvencies that followed the years of economic difficulty in the late 1870s. The effect of the drop in number of jobs was compounded by a drop

---

[8] It is typical of Craig Gardner's style at the time that 39 out of 90 jobs are not described — no time was wasted on management information of doubtful utility. Not until the 1950s was an attempt made in the Private Ledgers to separate fees and costs by type of work.
[9] *Thom's Directory* 1885.

in average fee per job, from £18 to £13, so that the fees recorded fell by nearly 50 per cent to £4651.[10] The charges allowed by the Courts had now risen to £3 3s per day for a principal, and £1 1s a day for an assistant; taking these as less than what would be generally charged by the firm, the average time spent on a job had gone down to one or two days for the principal and six or seven for an assistant.

In 1883/4 there were thirty-one jobs with a fee of more than £50, in 1885/6 only eleven. The 1883/4 jobs of more than £50 fees represented 5 per cent of the total, contributing 38 per cent of the recorded fees. Only two of the large 1883/4 jobs were also on the books in 1885/6; these were the Royal Bank (audit — £105) and the department store Arnott's (twice-yearly audit — £52). The Royal Bank was lost in the following year to Edward Kevans, a founder member of the Irish Society of Incorporated Accountants. Arnott's are still a client a hundred years later. Where they are described, most of the large jobs are liquidations, chancery accounts, or trust estates.

Throughout the 1880s, however, the firm did jobs for well-known commercial names, a few of whose business they have retained to this day. The range of clients was wide, though it is noticeable that the very largest Irish firms are not represented, either because they did not employ professional auditors at all, or because they used English firms. Perhaps also the very strong position the firm had in the liquidation and bankruptcy sector worked against it in the business field. In the commercial community,

[10] These figures are not the same as the firm's total turnover, since they are derived from the totals in the workbooks, and between 10 and 15 per cent of jobs have no fee listed; in a few cases, also, the fee actually paid is not the same as that originally noted. It is probable that the pattern of the 1870s, whereby a part of total turnover came from other sources, such as insurance agencies and investments, persisted. By the 1890s however, these sources had become insignificant, except for the occasional spectacular coup.

the memory was still green of the time when, as Maurice Brooks put it at the inaugural dinner of the Institute, 'the presence of an accountant was looked on in the same light as the visit of an undertaker or coroner would be.'[11]

Thus in banking the Royal (until 1886), the Belfast and the Provincial banks are listed in the workbooks, but not the Bank of Ireland, which eventually chose Deloitte's; various distilling and brewing companies such as Smithwicks and the Dublin Whisky Co. (founded in 1872), but not Guinness', Power's or Jameson's. In milling and baking the company worked for both Boland's and for the Ballsbridge company that was the eventual base for Johnston, Mooney and O'Brien; in railways, the West Clare Railway, and the Sallins and Baltinglass Railway and later the Strabane and Letterkenny Railway, but not, as we have seen, the very largest companies. In fact trams were more important, with the Dublin Tram Company, the Tramway Construction Company and other related concerns appearing on the books. Arnott's, Pim's and Fry's represented a good portfolio in the drapery business, but in chemicals the Dublin and Wicklow Manure Co. was clearly second to Goulding's.

In publishing the firm did occasional work for The Irish Times (perhaps making a connection through Sir John Arnott, who had bought the paper in 1874), but not for the Freeman's Journal; M.H. Gill were listed once in the 1870s, but not James Duffy or Hely's.

Outside the business arena the firm did regular work for hospitals (the Rotunda, Jervis St., Swift's, City of Dublin and the Coombe), for private clubs (the Turf, the Sackville St., the Royal St George, United Service) and for charities such as the non-sectarian Sick and Indigent Roomkeepers Society, at that time a major charity, providing relief to an average of 40,000 people a year. Like many of these

---

[11] *The Accountant* 1 December 1888.

organisations, the Sick and Indigent Society is still a client of the firm.

As far as can be judged from lists at the back of the 1882/3 and 1883/4 workbooks, all this work was done by Gardner and twenty-three or twenty-four clerks. The amount of practical supervision that Gardner himself could have been able to give to most of these jobs was obviously slight. The clerks appear to be organised into four groups, whose composition remains roughly the same from one year to the next. Of these twenty-four, only two, David Telford and John Gardner, Robert's son, became partners.

In 1886 two law cases added to the troubles caused by the drop in income. The first case, *In re O'Callaghan*,[12] arose out of an investigation that had been done in January 1884. John O'Callaghan was a wholesale grocer in Tralee. Through the solicitor Richard Davoren, Craig Gardner were asked to investigate the position of the business with a view to making an arrangement with the creditors. During the course of this investigation they received various sums of money on behalf of O'Callaghan. When O'Callaghan died in February 1884 the matter was turned into a bankruptcy. The official assignees in bankruptcy applied to Craig Gardner for all the money that they had received from the estate. Craig Gardner sent what they had received, less a sum for their costs.

The case turned on two points: firstly on whether Craig Gardner were entitled to deduct their fee at source, and how their costs were to be assessed, and secondly whether the work they had done on the case before it became a bankruptcy could be counted as having been done on behalf of the creditors. On appeal it was decided that all the work done could be charged according to the official scale of fees, and that Craig Gardner's should have credit for the amounts so ascertained to be properly payable in

---

[12] (1886) 19 Law Reports (Ireland) 32.

November 1883.

C. Furniss
D. Telford.
J. E. Russell.
R. McLeod.
J. McGeown.
D. McIntyre.
J. McGovern.
J. O'Callaghan.
J. McCracken.
D. Porter
W. Humphries
W. Barnes.
~~J. McArdle~~
J. A. Nairn
~~J. McGahey~~
A. Cuthbert
J. Honman.

H. Martin
R. Miller
R. Acheson.
J. Geary.
J. Gardner

J. Kelly.
J. O'Sullivan
J^s Russell.

The staff in 1883.

respect of costs and charges, and pay the balance into the court. The firm's work book for 1884 lists the total fee as £57 10s 8d, plus £5 for investigation.

The second case was more serious.[13] In February 1885 Daly and Co., a limited company with warehouses in Cork and Limerick, was near to collapse. The company Secretary approached Gardner, in his personal capacity, for a temporary accommodation to be repaid a month later when certain refinancing operations had been completed. As Gardner's affidavit put it 'after examining the accounts, for the purpose of saving the credit of the Company, pending the carrying out of the proposed plan for financing the company (which I believed would have been carried out) and to save the Company from being forced into liquidation in the meantime (which I believed would ultimately be avoided) I advanced the company the sum of £1500.'

Unfortunately the shareholders would not take up the new debentures, and the company was obliged to petition for voluntary winding-up. Gardner immediately requested the return of his money. There was some question between himself and the Secretary as to how the money was to be paid. Gardner was offered various customers' bills dated within two or three weeks, and the Secretary's evidence, which the judges accepted, was that he refused this method of payment, saying, 'I gave you cash and I want cash in the same way.' After this the Secretary, with the sanction of the Directors, paid Gardner back his money in cash. The records of the board's authorisation and the cheque payment were back-dated in the company's books to before the date of the petition for liquidation.

Not surprisingly, the transaction was treated by the courts as a fraudulent preference, and Gardner was ordered to repay the £1500. Nor did he come out of the case well

---

[13] *In re Daly & Co.* 19 Law Reports (Ireland) 16.

on a personal level: the Master of the Rolls described him as 'acting foolishly in parting with his money', and in the conflict of evidence between Gardner and the Secretary about the method of repayment, described the Secretary's account as 'much more probable and natural'.

Despite these setbacks, Robert Gardner and his firm were clearly the dominant force in the accountancy business in Ireland, and so naturally took the leading place in the establishment of the Institute of Chartered Accountants in Ireland.

Professional Status

The industrial revolution, and in particular the rise of large joint-stock companies, required more elaborate book- and office-learned skills than could be supplied by the generalist eighteenth-century 'man of business'. As a result groups of specialised workers — the professions — emerged to cope with various needs. At the beginning of the nineteenth century there were three qualifying professions in Ireland, the Church (meaning the Church of Ireland), the law (meaning the Bar) and medicine (meaning membership of the Royal College of Physicians). Membership of these groups conveyed the much sought-after designation of being a gentleman. Other groups, the lower professions, also existed, and to some extent regulated themselves; these included the apothecaries, the attorneys, and the surgeons. As the century progressed, these groups and others acquired qualifying status. Architects, engineers, and solicitors led the way, accountants followed, and finally specialisations such as company secretaries and patent agents were identifiable. One by one these groups sought to consolidate their position and their status by becoming publicly accredited. This activity was an important route by which the middle-classes in Europe secured their position as the dominant influence in the newly capitalistic economies.

By the late nineteenth century, the formula for an aspirant qualifying profession was well known. The usual start was for a group of the more respectable members of the would-be profession to gather together, motivated by a mixture of public and personal interest. The typical route to professional status thereafter would include making rules for the better running of the profession, establishing more or less rigorous entry requirements, setting up apprenticeship schemes, and establishing an Institute and a register of qualified practitioners. An inevitable feature was the establishment of a quasi-academic hierarchy, 'starting with students, probationers and Associates at the bottom and working up through Licentiates or Members to Fellows at the top, with honorary categories as required.'[14]

By adopting the old forms, the new organisations acquired instant respectability.

The next step was to seek external validation for what was until then merely a private club. The favoured choice was a Royal Charter, which brought its own prestige. Thus Irish solicitors were granted incorporation by Royal Charter in 1854, 24 years after the Law Society was founded, civil engineers in 1877, 42 years after their institute had been set up; architects had founded their Royal Society in 1839, which was incorporated in 1909. Another route, less favoured, was the setting up of an Irish branch of a British Institute; this was the path followed by the surveyors, who joined up with the London-based Royal Institute of Chartered Surveyors (incorporated in 1837).

The immediate impulse for the relatively late entry of English associations of accountants on the professionalising route was the need to identify qualified and experienced

---

[14] W.J. Reader *Professional Men: the rise of the professional classes in nineteenth century England* (London 1966) p 165.

practitioners following the deregulation of liquidation practice in the late 1860s. This opened the liquidation business, already expanding as a result of the vigorous creation and frequent collapse of limited liability companies, to a much wider market. Naturally the established professionals objected to the entry of competitors into their patch. Thus the Incorporated Society of Liverpool Accountants (the first professional accountancy body outside Scotland) was set up in 1870, as they put it, 'to weed the profession of a class of accountants or hedge-lawyers who have hitherto brought discredit on their order.'

The new professions often set very high entry standards in order to consolidate the position of its members. This was certainly the case with accountants, who had both practical and social reasons for maintaining exclusivity. The respectability of a profession depends to a large extent on how remunerative it is, but also on its practitioners being far removed from handling cash, which still carries the taint of 'trade'. Trollope describes how Dr Thorne, on his arrival in Barsetshire, got into trouble with his professional colleagues by at once announcing his scale of charges. They felt 'there was something low, mean and democratic in this . . . a physician ought to regard his pursuits in a purely philosophical spirit, and to have taken any gain which might have accrued as an accidental adjunct to his station in life.'[15] Accountancy, because of its subject matter, had problems in this regard that architects and actuaries could ignore. The new accountancy profession, both in England and Ireland, was therefore especially self-conscious about its entry requirements.

In later years, as accountants began to take over audits from nominated shareholders, status was important. In the

---

[15] A. Trollope *Doctor Thorne* (London 1858) Chapter III. To this day a barrister's gown contains a pocket at the back, into which clients are supposed surreptitiously to slip the great man's fees.

social climate professional and gentlemanly acceptability ran together, and clearly mere egalitarianism could not be allowed to set professional advancement at risk. As *The Accountant* put it some time later, when discussing the provision of accountancy education '[if the extra costs mean] that the course is only open to rich men and not the poor man . . . the matter is not of any consequence to the public . . . things may be made too easy for the impecunious man of ability.'[16]

This attitude, combined with a continuing growth in demand for trained accountancy staff, led more than once in the next fifty years to the founding of a new society with lesser prestige but also less stringent entry requirements than the one previously founded. Thus the Institute of Chartered Accountants of England and Wales was founded in 1880, and five years later the Society of Incorporated Accountants and Auditors was formed, made up of people who were not able to join the Institute. They were, as *The Accountant* patronisingly expressed it, 'a formidable array of clerks of all kinds — rent collectors, corn merchants, shop-keepers, valuers, collectors of taxes, bailiffs, secretaries of various concerns, civil engineers, school board clerks, overseers, timber agents, pawnbrokers and manure merchants.'[17]

It was this body which, by his account, approached Robert Stokes of Stokes Brothers and Pim in 1887 with a view to setting up an Irish branch. Stokes had been trained in Liverpool, where the first Incorporated Society had been set up in 1870. Stokes called a meeting of the leading Irish accountants, and it was decided instead to set up their own organisation and to attempt to obtain a Charter. This was not in fact the first time that such ideas had been mooted.[18]

[16] *The Accountant* 11 November 1911.
[17] *The Accountant* 20 March 1886.
[18] The story of the early days of the Institute is based on H. Robinson *A History of Accountants in Ireland* 2nd edn (Dublin 1983).

Eventually a petition was drawn up, signed by thirteen accountants from Dublin, twelve from Belfast and six from Cork. The Dublin group included at least five with Craig Gardner connections, viz. Robert Gardner and his son John, ex-employees John Cunningham and Patrick O'Harte, and Henry Brown. In the smaller Cork group was William Atkins, whose firm Atkins, Chirnside merged with Craig Gardner in 1975. The petition was accepted, and the Royal Charter, dated 14 May 1888, was granted. Robert Gardner became the first President. The inauguration was celebrated with a great dinner, where Robert Gardner declared that 'much may be done to elevate the profession of which we are members and much may be done to increase the respect and confidence which is at present extended to us by the legal profession and the general public in Ireland.' It is clear that the legal profession is still the major focus of accountants' attention: it was noted that 'practically the whole legal profession' responded to Gardner's invitation, which was seen as a tribute to his 'personal weight and social influence as one of the leading citizens of Dublin, irrespective of his position as head of his firm.'[19]

The first general meeting of the Irish Institute took place in the office of Craig Gardner at Trinity Chambers on 19 November 1888. Thirty-one members and the solicitor Thomas Fitzgerald attended. The main object of the meeting was to approve the Bye-Laws, which was speedily done. The second item on the agenda, the question as to whether members of the new Institute should be allowed to advertise, was not so easily disposed of. Victorian advertising was generally of a brash, unsubtle quality, in which techniques suitable for promoting professional services were scarcely distinguished from those appropriate

---

[19] *The Accountant* 1 December 1888 — there were at least fourteen speeches during the course of the dinner.

Three of the partners in 1890: Robert Gardner (left), *John Gardner* (below) *and David Telford* (right).

to soap or patent medicines. The early Brown, Craig announcements may have been effective, but they were scarcely dignified. This lack of gentlemanly dignity made advertising one of the yardsticks by which the Victorians distinguished a profession from a trade. As *The Accountant* put it in a discussion of the Irish debate, 'no medical professional man advertises — quacks do, which is one point of difference.' Another inducement to forbidding advertising for established members of the profession was that it would enhance the status of accountants in the eyes of the world and in particular in the eyes of their main contacts: 'the practice has become a nuisance and a scandal; and has long been a source of amusement to Irish legal practitioners.'[20]

In economic terms the ban on advertising was attractive to the existing firms, making it harder in a limited market for smaller companies to expand their businesses, or for new entrants to win clients. In the long run, the prohibition of advertising stimulated the practice whereby a man wishing to set up his own firm took clients with him when he left the firm where he had his professional formation. Because the relations between audit seniors and clients were always likely to be closer than between the partner and the clients, this was difficult to prevent. Under Robert Gardner, the firm had not in fact been enthusiastic advertisers, for though they regularly took space in *Thom's Directory* and the *Law Society's Yearbook*, the wording of these advertisements was identical year after year. When the issue came up in the new-fledged Institute, Gardner took a strong line, and the practice was forbidden.

Unfortunately this promising start was not, at least as far as Craig Gardner was concerned, maintained. In 1889 Robert Gardner was instrumental in bringing together three of the bigger bakers in Dublin to form the Ballsbridge

---

[20] *The Accountant* 11 November 1888.

company of Johnston, Mooney and O'Brien. His second wife, Jane, had inherited the Johnston company on the death of her father, but clearly neither Gardner nor she wanted to run a large bakery company. He therefore approached two of the other large bakery companies, and registered the combined company in November 1888. Technically, Gardner, Mooney and the O'Brien brothers actually sold their individual companies to David Telford, an assistant in Craig Gardner, representing the new company. Gardner and his wife received £72,500 for Johnston's, made up of £43,500 cash and the rest in shares.

The Memorandum and Articles of Association of the new company stated:
'143. At least once in every year the accounts of the Company shall be examined, and the correctness of the balance sheet ascertained by one or more auditors.
144. The first auditors shall be Messrs Cooper Brothers...'

Unfortunately this employment of English accountants hit a raw nerve among Irish accountants, who were very conscious of the overshadowing power of British firms and their ability to take the best Irish audits. The placing of the audit of Guinness' with Turquand, Young in London after its public flotation in 1886 was a typical case where the experience of City of London accountancy firms had prevailed. This was incidentally an experience that Irish accountants shared with their American colleagues, who were equally overshadowed by firms originating in the City of London. Large amounts of British capital had been exported to the US, and English and Scottish accountancy firms, sent to monitor the progress of these investments, were prominent there, especially on the eastern seaboard.

The Council of the new Institute expressed its annoyance at the involvement of Cooper Brothers by holding a special meeting. Gardner sent a note saying 'he thought it better that he should not attend as he was personally interested.' The meeting passed a resolution stating that they felt that Gardner's action 'in calling in the assistance of English accountants to investigate the accounts in a purely Irish matter, and their subsequent appointment as auditors to the limited company formed after such investigation is very prejudicial to the interests of the Institute and unfair to its members . . .' It is not clear from the records why Gardner did not use his own firm. Perhaps the fact that Johnston's affairs were after all strictly his wife's business rather than his own may have been at the bottom of it.

It appears that the committee sent this resolution to the newspapers without ensuring that a copy reached Gardner first. There was even a suggestion, as expressed by An Onlooker in *The Accountant*, that 'this was done for the purpose of injuring his firm with the "patriotic" section of the public.'[21] Tradition has it that when Gardner read the report in the paper he was so annoyed that he took a heavy inkwell and hurled it through a window on which had recently been painted 'Craig, Gardner and Co., Chartered Accountants'. He immediately wrote tendering his resignation both from the Presidency and from the Institute itself, and stuck to his decision, despite various attempts to make him change his mind. He never rejoined the Institute, though he took part in various activities from as early as 1893.

The Accountant described this whole affair as one of 'kicking the lion, under the idea they were dealing with an ass . . .', and if other members of Craig Gardner had not stayed in the Institute, the precipitate departure of the principal of the largest firm in the country might have had serious consequences for the organisation of the profession in Ireland. As it was, because all the partners were not members of the Institute, the firm was no longer able to describe itself as 'Chartered Accountants' until Gardner's retirement. The firm's letterhead therefore used the rubric

---

[21] *The Accountant* 28 December 1889.

'Auditors and Accountants'. Gardner remained a director of Johnston, Mooney and O'Brien until 1918.

Luckily the firm had other representatives in the Institute, and three of them, David Telford, William Harris and John Gardner (Robert's son) became partners within a few months of Robert Gardner's resignation from the Institute, in October 1890. The deed gave each of the new partners a salary of £300, and then a share of profits as follows: David Telford — $\frac{1}{6}$; John Gardner — $\frac{1}{12}$; and William Harris — $\frac{1}{12}$. Robert Gardner was to have $\frac{2}{3}$ share of profits and no salary. All the capital and the rights in the name remained his. Telford, who had been with the firm since the seventies, and was later to become senior partner, is clearly seen as the most valuable of the new men; John Gardner is put on a par with Harris, a relatively recent recruit, who had joined the staff some time after 1883.

CHAPTER 3

'AUDITORS AND ACCOUNTANTS'
1890-1904

B etween 1889 and 1891 Ireland's most famous political leader, Charles Stewart Parnell, struggled to save his career, and with it the hopes of a peaceful parliamentary solution to the Irish problem. The fall of Parnell, who died aged only 45 in October 1891, was also the end of an era. Irish parliamentary politics became bogged down for fifteen years in squabbles between pro- and anti-Parnellite factions. This left the field clear for various forms of non-parliamentary nationalism.

These nationalists generally sought an Ireland that was Gaelic, Catholic, and above all separate from England. Part of the mix of ideas was a recoil from the modern that was widely felt throughout Europe; de Valera's much derided St Patrick's Day broadcast in 1942, in which he spoke of his vision of Ireland as a non-materialist, rural civilisation, was merely a late flowering of this mood. In Ireland the modern was represented by England, seen as rich, domineering, and pagan (or what was virtually the same thing, Protestant). Irish clerics, poets and nationalists vied with each other in extravagant denunciations of everything from over the water, from its godless culture to 'England's stuffs and broadcloths and such other effeminate follies', as Archbishop Croke put it. Douglas Hyde, founder of the Gaelic League, railed against the aping of English dress, and proposed kneebreeches as the ideal native male dress.[1] In this climate, accountancy was clearly identified with the modern movement, with the despised 'Manchesterism', as well as being, like so much else in the business world, largely Protestant-controlled, and part of what Yeats called 'the shoddy society of West Britonism'.

The new atmosphere often seemed exasperatingly small-minded, as when in 1899 children from National Schools were forbidden to attend a Breakfast in the Phoenix Park

---

[1] T. Garvin 'Priests and Patriots: Irish separatism and the fear of the modern 1890-1914' in *Irish Historical Studies* vol xxv no. 67 (May 1986).

to celebrate Queen Victoria's visit. This was on the grounds that the Ladies Committee of Catholics and Protestants who had organised the breakfast were engaged in 'political souperism', and a 'mean, transparent plot' to 'undermine the National spirit of the rising generation' by associating the Queen with a day off school, and a liberal supply of cakes and jam. The cakes and jam were provided by, among others, Craig Gardner clients Johnston, Mooney and O'Brien (3,000 buns) and Williams and Woods (one ton of jam and 10,000 bags of sweets).[2] For Craig Gardner's this change in the political and social mood had implications for the development of the firm — how was the new atmosphere likely to affect a business that was comfortably identified with the existing regime?

In fact the business community, especially in the banks, the professions and the larger businesses, was still dominated by Protestants, and was to remain so for long after Independence. For the Craig Gardner partners, moving from the largely Protestant areas of the Rathmines and Pembroke townships (the Gardners lived in Pembroke, Telford in Rathmines and Harris in Harold's Cross) to the equally Protestant environs of Dame Street, it must have been easy to suppress any urge for radical change. In the event the firm did not admit a Catholic partner until 1944. On the other hand there is no evidence of discrimination against Catholics or even republicans in the lower ranks, as the recruitment of the militants Michael Collins, Joe McGrath and Joe Considine shows. (Of course it is unlikely that political allegiance was much discussed during the recruitment interviews, and the partners' reaction would undoubtedly have been different had they known just how deeply these men were involved.) David Telford's secretary in later years, Miss Webb, was an ex-nun. There is however no reason to doubt that the

---

[2] J. McCarthy *Five Years in Ireland* (Dublin 1901) pp 484-6 and Appendix B.

partners, with the rest of the business community, favoured the Union, seeing it as a bulwark of economic and political stability, and a support for the Protestant religion.

This was the era of which C.S. Andrews wrote 'from childhood I was aware that there were two separate and immiscible kinds of citizens: the Catholics, of whom I was one, and the Protestants, who were as remote and different from us as if they had been blacks and we whites.'[3] Protestant orphanages were particular objects of Catholic suspicion, not always unreasonably. One Craig Gardner client, the Rev. Cotton and his wife, ran the Caragh Orphanage, near Naas, which came under suspicion of cruelty in the 1880s. Cotton was tried in 1891 for what the *Leinster Leader* called 'barbarous ill-treatment inflicted upon helpless children in the notorious institution'; among the punishments inflicted was that of 'logging' which involved padlocking a log of wood to the child's leg, perhaps for several days and nights. At the trial Craig Gardners reported that the finances of the orphanage were satisfactory, but the 'home' was closed, and Cotton sent to prison.[4]

Protestants did not however form the homogenous social and political group imagined by Catholic polemicists. There was a considerable difference in political and social attitudes between the Church of Ireland's adherents and other groups. The original Craig Gardner partners were not of the ascendancy, Church of Ireland, set. As in England, where many of the founders of the great accountancy firms such as William Cooper (a Quaker), William Deloitte (from a Catholic family), Edwin Waterhouse (born a Presbyterian) and Samuel Price (Waterhouse's partner — a Baptist) were not Anglicans, so also in Ireland. Robert Gardner came from the solidly northern Presbyterian linen town of Ballymoney, County Antrim, and David Telford

[3] C.S. Andrews *Dublin Made Me* (Dublin 1979) p 9.
[4] *Leinster Leader* 4 August 1984.

from an evangelical settlement in the same county, where he later bought a house and farm.

Telford remained all his life a member of the Moravians, or United Brethren, who had established a settlement in Gracehill near Ballymena in 1746, after fleeing from their original home in central Europe. Gracehill was a small place, only 39 families (326 people) in 1837, with separate houses for unmarried men and unmarried women. The Moravians were bible Christians who believed in controlling their lives (even to their choice of marriage partner) by the casting of lots, though as one author put it, not everything was left to chance: 'the questions put to the lot were so skilfully varied in wording, with so many alternatives and overlaps that the considered opinion of the Elders was not often rejected...'[5] Their other notable eccentricity, apart from a distaste for theological wrangling, was in burying their dead upright. By 1906 there were a mere 6,300 Moravians in the British Isles, and some 20,000 in the US.

In their clubs too, the partners kept their distance from the high ascendancy. Gardner was a member of the Stephen's Green Club and the Royal Irish Yacht Club (where the Findlaters were also members), rather than the more establishment Kildare Street and Royal St George options. In a book of contemporary biographies, Telford gave the Corinthian (a dining club founded in 1897 by the city's Chief Medical Officer of Health Sir Charles Cameron) and Portmarnock Golf as his clubs.

Several of the partners undoubtedly became Freemasons; as prominent Protestant figures in Dublin business life, it would have been surprising if at least some had not. The first partner to join was David Telford, who was initiated in 1894 into the small Howth Lodge, where he lived at that

---

[5] Jenks *The Moravian Brethren in North Wales* quoted in R.A. Knox *Enthusiasm* (Oxford 1950).

time.⁶ In 1902, long after he had ceased to be concerned with actively building the business, Robert Gardner was initiated into the Duke of York Lodge No. 25. This was the premier commercial Lodge in Dublin, with over 200 members, including some important business people. The Lodge was dominated by the indefatigably clubbable Sir Charles Cameron, with whom Gardner would have come in contact in connection with the affairs of Pembroke urban district council, to which he had been elected in January 1902. They were powerful fundraisers, on one occasion (no doubt after a particularly good dinner) donating more for a particular charity than all of the rest of the city lodges together.

Twenty-five new members joined this Lodge in the same year as Gardner, including ten army officers, three barristers, a manager, a civil servant, a land agent, a doctor and a company secretary. Three years later Gardner became first Junior Warden of a much smaller new lodge (No. 395) in 1905, of which he became Master in 1908. He does not appear to have held any Grand Office, nor was he a foreign representative. He is not mentioned in the obituaries in the Grand Lodge Report, so it is likely that he did not take a very active role in the Order.

In 1921 Eustace Shott, who became a partner in 1924, joined Lodge No. 399, among whose other members were some engineers, a commercial representative, a railway clerk, a brewery foreman, an auctioneer, a civil servant and a clerk.⁷ Shott resigned from the Order in 1931, at the time when his contribution to the business-getting side of the firm's activity

---

⁶ The information about masonic membership is derived from the archives of the Order by permission of Archivist, Mr Charles Horton.
⁷ These job descriptions cannot totally be relied on — Shott himself, who was in articles at the time of his application, is listed in the indexes and the main lodge record (though not in the Charity Book) as a civil servant.

133 Dr. — Profit & Loss

1898			Forward		2615	16	7
Mar 31	To Salaries			124	5512	4	5
"	" Furniture			7	55	4	
"	" R Gardner	R Gardner		2	1900	3	10
"	" D Telford	D Telford		10	633	4	10
"	" W Harris	W Harris		13	633	4	10
"	" J Gardner	J Gardner		16	633	4	10
					16190		5
99 Mar 31	" Subscriptions			271	42	18	
"	" Charges, Rent, Income Tax &c			107	1293	15	7
"	" Salaries			125	5847	15	6
"	" R Gardner	R Gardner		2	3573	3	7
"	" D Telford	D Telford		10	1191	1	3
"	" W Harris	W Harris		13	1191	1	2
"	" J Gardner	J Gardner		16	1191	1	2
1900					14330	16	3
Mar 31	" Bad Debt Pakenham			419	1024	15	11
"	" Subscriptions			272	101	8	
"	" Charges Rent Income Tax &c			108	1337	16	6
"	" Salaries			125	6199	7	1
"	" R Gardner	R Gardner		3	7274	4	1
"	" D Telford	D Telford		10	2424	14	8
"	" W Harris	W Harris		13	2424	14	8
"	" J Gardner	J Gardner		16	2424	14	9
					23211	15	8

Contra — Cr. 133

1898		Forward			1,376	15	9	
Mar 31	By Reconstruction A/c		255	21,391	15	3	
"	" Avondale Hotel Co		266	1006	8	5	
"	" R & J Hill		141	6787	12	1	
"	" Waring & Gillow		154	2564	17	11	
"	" Fee Account		86	13062	15	7	
				46190	5		
1899							
Mch 31	" Discount & Sundries		418	762	2	8	
"	" London Office		231	1042	8	7	
"	" Fee Account		86	13212	5		
				4,330	16	3	
1900							
Mar 31	" London Office		235	7457	11	11	
"	" Discount & Sundries		420	95	6	4	
"	" London Office Charges A/c 10:11		13	61	3	6	
"	" Fee Account		87	15597	13	11	
				23211	15	8	

The Private Ledger, in David Telford's hand, showing the distribution of the great profits of 1898 and the lesser amounts for 1899 and 1900.

was just starting to be significant. The next partner to join the Masons was William Cunningham, who joined on his marriage in 1940, largely, by his own account, for the social and welfare benefits.

It is difficult to see anything sinister in this. None of the partners were members of important lodges at any key business-getting times. It is unlikely that any business (except possibly the audits of a few small charities) resulted from the partners' membership. The situation described in one Catholic Truth Society pamphlet — 'the Masonic lodges of Ireland . . . thrive on secrecy and underhand ways, plotting unfair advantage over their rivals in industry, trade and commerce'[8] — simply didn't exist, at least for Craig Gardner. The fact that it was generally believed to exist, however, no doubt led to the active lobbying style employed by the Knights of St Columbanus, which was to affect the firm adversely in the 1920s and 1930s.

The new partnership started with a very good year. Fee income amounted to £17,543 in the year ending 28 February 1891. After salaries and expenses, the partners had a comfortable sum of very nearly £13,000 after tax to share, of which Robert Gardner's two-thirds came to £8,655, twice the average annual earnings of a leading barrister at that time.[9] During the rest of the 1890s, fee income never went above £10,000, and in fact this record was not to be approached again until the inflationary days of 1921 and 1922. From the private ledger it appears that the success

---

[8] Rev. G. Clune *Freemasonry — Its Origins, Aims and Methods* (Dublin 1931).
[9] W. O'Connor Morris, a County Court Judge, wrote in his memoirs in 1895 that 'the incomes made at the Irish Bar are very much less than at the English; from £3,000 to £5,000 a year are the highest sums, I should say, in private practice.' Quoted in D. Hogan *The Legal Profession in Ireland 1789-1922* (Dublin 1986) p 82.

was not just a matter of one exceptionally good account. Fees furnished in April, June, August and December were all higher than they were to be again for years.

The unusually high earnings were no doubt connected with the launch as public companies in 1890 of Craig Gardner clients Switzers, Dublin & Wicklow Manure, Alexander Thom & Co., Crowe Wilson and the Castlebellingham & Drogheda Brewery. A contributory factor may have been the crisis caused by the collapse of the city of London bankers Barings, which caused what the Governor of the Bank of Ireland described as 'a period of great anxiety' and a 'general depression of business', but since this crisis only broke in November 1890, its impact would have come only late in the year.

The 1890s as a whole, taking advantage of the recovery in trade in the late 1880s, showed remarkable activity in the number of launches of public companies. Apart from those already mentioned, other Craig Gardner clients to go into the market in the decade included: drapers Crowe Wilson in 1890, wholesale warehousemen Ferrier Pollock in 1891, wine and spirit merchants Bagots Hutton in 1894, seedsmen W. Drummond & Co in 1895, and in 1896 tea merchants Baker Wardell, with Drogheda Chemicals, and the reconstructed Dublin United Tramways (1896) Ltd. In all some forty major companies were launched on the Dublin stock exchange between 1888 and 1897, and the total registrations of new limited companies ran from some fifty new companies a year in the 1880s to as many as 145 in 1897. The quoted capital on the Dublin stock exchange went from £7.25m at the beginning of the decade to £17.2m at the end.[10]

The firm's level of earnings in 1890 was not however repeated in the subsequent years of the century, during

[10] W. Thomas *The Stock Exchanges of Ireland* (Liverpool 1986) pp 145, 153, 262-3.

which annual fee income averaged £11,500, fluctuating between £8,000 in 1895 and just under £15,000 in 1897. Clearly the firm was still largely dependent on the 'once-off' business that had been the pattern since 1875. In fact it is not until 1904 that this erratic pattern settles down. By that time a new mix of business appears to have been achieved. The steady growth of audit work, repeating year after year, was thereafter the core source of income, with liquidations, secretarial and trust work providing what extra they could. This pattern is echoed in the records of accountancy firms in the City of London, where the fluctuations in earnings caused by large, one-off insolvencies begins to be damped by the 1890s, as audit work contributes more than 50 per cent of the fees.[11]

A Craig Gardner workbook dating from the late 1890s,[12] detailing expected work month by month, shows the growing importance of the audit business. It lists just over two hundred jobs in this recurrent capacity, between a third and half of the total workload. Of the 209 jobs listed, only a quarter were also listed in the workbooks of ten years before. The market had changed. By 1901 there were 1,120 limited companies registered in Ireland, according to the directory compiled by the accountant Michael Crowley. The total paid-up capital of all companies was £34.7m.[13] A Craig Gardner client, Dublin United Tramways, had the largest paid-up capital (£1.2m.), but in most cases even the authorised share capital did not exceed £250,000.

From surviving audit reports it is clear that the firm often took a wide view of its responsibilities as auditors.

---

[11] See E. Jones *Accountancy and the British Economy 1840-1980* (London 1981) Chapter 4.
[12] The book is not dated, but can certainly be placed after 1894, since it includes the Irish Agricultural Organisation Society, which was founded in March of that year. For a full list of the clients noted in this book, see Appendix 2.
[13] Michael Crowley *Directory and Statistics of Limited Liability Companies registered in Ireland* (Dublin 1901).

In a long letter to the Board of McBirney's dated February 1891, for instance, the firm analysed the gross profits of several departments in an attempt to identify the causes of an overall gross profit drop. The firm also complained that McBirney's allowance of only £1,000 bad debt reserve on £20,000 of debts was too small — 'we have to express the hope that the collection of accounts is well looked after', as they commented somewhat tartly.

The anonymous partner's letter also criticised the shop's rate of stock-turn: 'we do not think that this turnover is sufficiently rapid. It ought to be turned over 4 or 5 times at least and we greatly fear that to this cause can be attributed the fact of old or depreciated stock which you have been compelled to write off in the present half [-year]. We think your buyers should be asked to keep their stocks lower, and to turn them over oftener so as to keep them clean and fresh.' Finally they complained about the 6 per cent dividend the directors proposed to pay: 'we are strongly of the opinion that you would be acting wisely if you limited the dividend on the ordinary shares to 5 per cent. We think this policy of paying a slightly smaller dividend is a much wiser one having regard to the large amount of debts outstanding and to the fact that your lease is running out very quickly.' The Minutes of the Board meeting which considered this letter, along with other responses, noted dryly, 'the Directors resolved to pay 6 per cent, after a careful consideration of the matter.'[14]

In a report dated December 1899 to the directors of Monica Duff & Co. Ltd, a large general store in Ballaghaderreen, Co. Mayo, John Gardner for the firm is equally blunt: the 'profit is equivalent to only three per cent on the sales, which having regard to the nature of the commodities is perfectly absurd . . . we estimate that a profit of between

---

[14] The McBirney's minute book is in the Business Records section of the Public Record Office.

£3,000 and £4,000 at least should have been earned . . . in these circumstances we are led to conclude that goods or the proceeds of goods to a very large extent are unaccounted for, and by a casual examination which we have made of past accounts we fear that this unsatisfactory state of affairs has existed for a considerable time.' Four years later Craig Gardner's were still not happy. 'We still entertain the opinion that dishonesty in some shape or form has been the cause of the serious deficiency shown by the Accounts . . .'[15]

In the 1890s workbook seventy clients are specifically listed as being limited companies, and many more (such as the West Clare Railway, the Dundalk Patent Slip Co., and the Hibernian Plate Glass Insurance Co.) undoubtedly were. Among the big audits (with their annual fees) are Arnott's (£105), Belfast Banking (£157), E. & J. Burke Ltd (international wine and spirit merchants: £210 — the top fee), Dublin Distillers (£200), Ferrier, Pollock (£90), Johnston, Mooney & O'Brien (£200), Provincial Bank (£89) Junior Army and Navy Stores (£100), and Irish Civil Service Building Society (£70). E. & J. Burke had been incorporated in 1891 and the Chairman boasted in 1902 that in the twelve years since then they had generated profits of nearly one million pounds sterling.[16] They remained Craig Gardner clients for many years, though by 1906 they were audited by Craig Gardner and Harris in London.

Twenty-seven fees are recorded £50 or more, and these contribute over half of the recorded income. The average for the 209 jobs listed in Craig Gardner's workbook of the late 1890s was £29. At this time the wages of a craftsman,

---

[15] Shortly after this, two employees were let go, and margins returned to more conventional levels. The originals of these documents are in the possession of John Blake Dillon, a Craig Gardner partner since 1976, whose grandfather owned the company.
[16] *The Irish Times* 4 June 1902.

such as a printer, were about £90 a year in Dublin,[17] so the average Dublin fee represented one-third the annual earnings of a skilled worker.

Many of the jobs involved multiple visits to the firm during the year, at six-monthly, three-monthly or in some cases monthly intervals. Thus the druggists Boileau and Boyd, the Dublin United Tramways, Dockrells, the Irish Civil Service Building Society, the IAOS and the shipowners Palgrave, Murphy were all visited monthly. Seventy-eight firms were visted twice in a year, including the stores, the warehousing companies, and the railways. The twice-yearly accounting process was quite usual in commercial firms at this time. Craig Gardner's themselves made up their accounts twice-yearly in the 1870s, and for the railways it was a statutory requirement. In general these were proper period end audits, not interim audits, in which all the books would be closed off and a profit and loss account drawn up. This double activity in the year was of course only practical in a fairly simple accounting and auditing environment.

The private ledger records the structure of the firm's income and expenditure at this time. For the 1890s, salaries ran at 40 per cent of fee income, other costs (including subscriptions and a line called 'Rent, income tax, and charges') at 10 per cent, leaving the partners' profits at 50 per cent. This is apparently a very normal result. One contemporary writer gives a typical breakdown of costs and profit for a two partner firm in London as being: salaries 36 per cent of fee income, rent 7 per cent, other costs 7 per cent and partners' profit 50 per cent.[18]

This is of course in relation to ordinary fee income. The income of Craig Gardner was not however always limited to this. In 1898, for instance, the extraordinary

[17] M. Daly *Dublin — the Deposed Capital* (Cork 1984) p 69.
[18] W. Fox *Accountants' Accounts* (London 1888).

sum of £33,127 (two and half times that year's actual fee income) was taken into profits and distributed to the partners. Robert Gardner's share of this was £19,003, only just less than the whole annual income of the Royal Dublin Society, then in its heyday. This sum appears to be the result of company launches, and investment in these companies. This seems to have been a regular practice. Thus Gardner's capital account in the private ledger shows investments in Dockrells debentures (£1000 in 1891), McEnnery Bros (£5320 in 1894, a year after registration as a public company), Phoenix Brewery (£1000 in 1897), Beeston Brewery (a Nottingham company floated in 1896 — £2785 in 1897) and so on. All of these were in one way or another clients — this form of insider trading was to remain quite normal for many years.

The Phoenix Brewery had been floated in 1896, with a prospectus prepared by Craig Gardner showing profits of £18,000 a year. Unfortunately the following year the company lost the lucrative army contract, and by 1899 had lost £12,000 in eighteen months. The shareholders were not pleased, and appointed an accountant to look into the matter, and especially to report on the prospectus. In the end, as the *Irish Investor's Guardian* reported 'Craig Gardner have been fully and entirely vindicated, while the "base and foul" accusations, formulated as a result of Mr Finnegan's "expert" examination of the accounts, against these gentlemen has recoiled with telling force on the head of the accusers.'[19]

A month later the journal returned to the controversy with some revealing, if optimistic, remarks about contemporary professional practice. 'Surely settled principles govern an audit of even brewery accounts, and it is not left to any accountant to say how much or how little should be set aside. The old idea of "what side do you want the balance?" does not now obtain. Auditors have become

[19] October 1899.

independent. They are the servants of the Shareholders and not the tools of the Directors as was their wont in the good old times when the principles of commercial rectitude were not placed under the fierce light of public criticism to the extent that now obtains.'

Against this high note must be set the state of affairs Craig Gardner found in 1906 in the course of an investigation into the affairs of the Irish Provident Assurance Co., a company with a revenue account of £75,000: 'we found the book-keeping in existence ... unsatisfactory and that the financial position of the company could not be readily ascertained therefrom ... further there appeared to be no books from which all items in the previous balance sheet could be identified and traced to their source.'

The Belfast and London Offices

In 1894 one of Craig Gardner's partners, William Harris, came into conflict with the Institute. Harris was a remarkable man. He was born in the Isle of Man and joined a Manchester firm of accountants as office boy at the age of 14, on a wage of 6/- a week. Five years later he was offered free articles, an unheard-of privilege (it was said that he never forgot this, and always refused to take a premium for pupils himself). At the end of his five years service he gained first place in the Finals and First Certificate of Merit. He joined Craig Gardner's a year later, in 1888, and was offered a partnership in 1890, at the age of 27. He was a specialist in brewery accounts, and published a book on the topic in 1892. He was also one of the first leader writers for *The Accountant*.[20]

---

[20] His obituary was printed in *The Accountant* 3 November 1923.

A member of the Irish Institute since 1889, Harris complained to the Council in January 1894 that Stokes Brothers and Pim had breached professional etiquette. They had accepted the audit of a firm which had refused to circulate to the shareholders a qualification to the accounts asked for by Harris. The firm, The Official Guide Ltd, had been a Craig Gardner client for many years when disputes arose in the early 1890s.

In 1893 Harris insisted that the accounts record that the debtors figure 'includes a number of accounts, some of which are absolutely bad, and others which are extremely doubtful' as well as two other objections relating to stock valuation 'at more than cost price' and items that should have been written off. This was not the first time that the firm had complained to the Directors about the accounts. Having refused to circulate the note in full, the Directors proposed that Stokes Brothers be elected auditors, which they duly were. In February 1894 the Council of the Institute accepted that Stokes had not touted for the business, and were quite at liberty to accept the work, and 'had not infringed the letter or the spirit of the Charter and Bye Laws of the Institute'. Harris at once resigned from the Institute, and in due course went to London to set up a Craig Gardner office there. Dr Robinson expresses a modern practitioner's view of this transaction: 'it would seem to a disinterested observer... that Craig Gardner were justified in their refusal to give a clear certificate.'[21]

The coincidence, of Harris's accession to partnership and the commencement of disputes with this long-time client, is striking. In truth, Gardner would have been able to exercise only very slight personal supervision over the hundreds of jobs that were billed every year, and so it is highly likely that the clerk allocated to the

---

[21] *A History of Accountants in Ireland* 2nd edn (Dublin 1983) p 93, from which this account is taken.

Dame Street in the early 1900s.

job simply accepted whatever had been done the previous year as correct, a position a keen new partner would be unlikely to adopt.

By the 1890s corporate business, both in launches and audits, had largely replaced the old insolvency service. It was therefore desirable to establish a presence in Belfast and London, where much of the action was. The greatest number of limited companies registered in Ireland were based in Ulster, including over 100 linen companies; no doubt as a result Belfast seems to have been the first office set up. A deed dated 25 April 1896 notes that Edward Buckley had been Craig Gardner's clerk in charge there since 1894. By the deed Buckley is confirmed in the post as manager of the Belfast branch, at a salary of £204 per annum, rising to £256 by 1901. In December 1901 Buckley was made a partner in the Belfast business, on a salary of £250 plus one-fifth of the net profits. His territory was defined as the 'Province of Ulster', except for those clients who were already handled from the Dublin or London offices. Any Belfast staff time used by these offices was to be credited.

The accounts in the Private Ledger show that the average contribution for the first ten years of this arrangement was just over £800, which, with Buckley's profit share added back and a gross profit rate of 50 per cent assumed, gives the office a turnover of just over £2,000 a year. At this time the Belfast office employed three out of the seven English chartered accountants employed in Belfast. After 1913 profits contributed to Dublin took a decided upward turn, reaching £4,479 by 1922. During the same period, the Dublin office's gross fees doubled from £9,500 to £18,000. Unlike the Belfast growth, which was steady throughout the war period, the main growth in Dublin fees, from £11,500 to £18,000, was during the period of high inflation and economic boom in the South between 1917 and 1920.

In 1909 a further deed of partnership relating to the Belfast operation was signed, this time by Sir Robert Gardner, as he had become, David Telford, and John Gardner, giving

Buckley a 50 per cent share in the Belfast business. The deed was witnessed by G.H. Tulloch, Chartered Accountant, who next year became a partner himself, and eventually was to be senior partner.

The other venture into branch offices was London, which was managed by William Harris. This first appears in the books in 1897, when the branch office is recorded as having a cash balance of £376. A profit contribution is recorded separately from 1899, starting at just over a £1,000, and leaping to £7,500 in 1900. In 1902 the contribution dropped to £470, but five years later the contribution had steadied at over £2,000, and was rising.

A profit and loss statement for the year ended 31 March 1900 shows that the London office was handling company formations in quite a big way. The firm seems to have been extremely successful, particularly in new company launches, which in England were running at the rate of over 4,000 a year in the decade before the First World War. For instance, Harris was involved in the launch of the new Carlton Hotel in 1898, with the great French chef Escoffier as the main attraction, and the Welsbach Incandescent Company, which had the patent for the newly invented gas mantles, which 'staved off the doom of gas as an illuminant' for several decades after the development of electric lighting.[22] In 1900 the launch of Henderson Brothers appears to have grossed £10,197, and the Ashby Staines Brewery underwriting £1,000. Total income for the year amounted to £15,463, including £3,149 of audit fees.

Until 1903 the business was run by William Harris as a branch office of Craig Gardner's in Dublin. In that year Harris left the Dublin and Belfast partnerships, and a new arrangement was made for London. This involved a

---

[22] The Welsbach mantle replaced the yellow gas flare, which 'heated the air, blackened the ceilings and gave only a moderate degree of illumination for a great expenditure of gas', Derry and Williams *A Short History of Technology* (Oxford 1960) p 513.

NET FEES FOR THE THREE OFFICES 1899-1910*

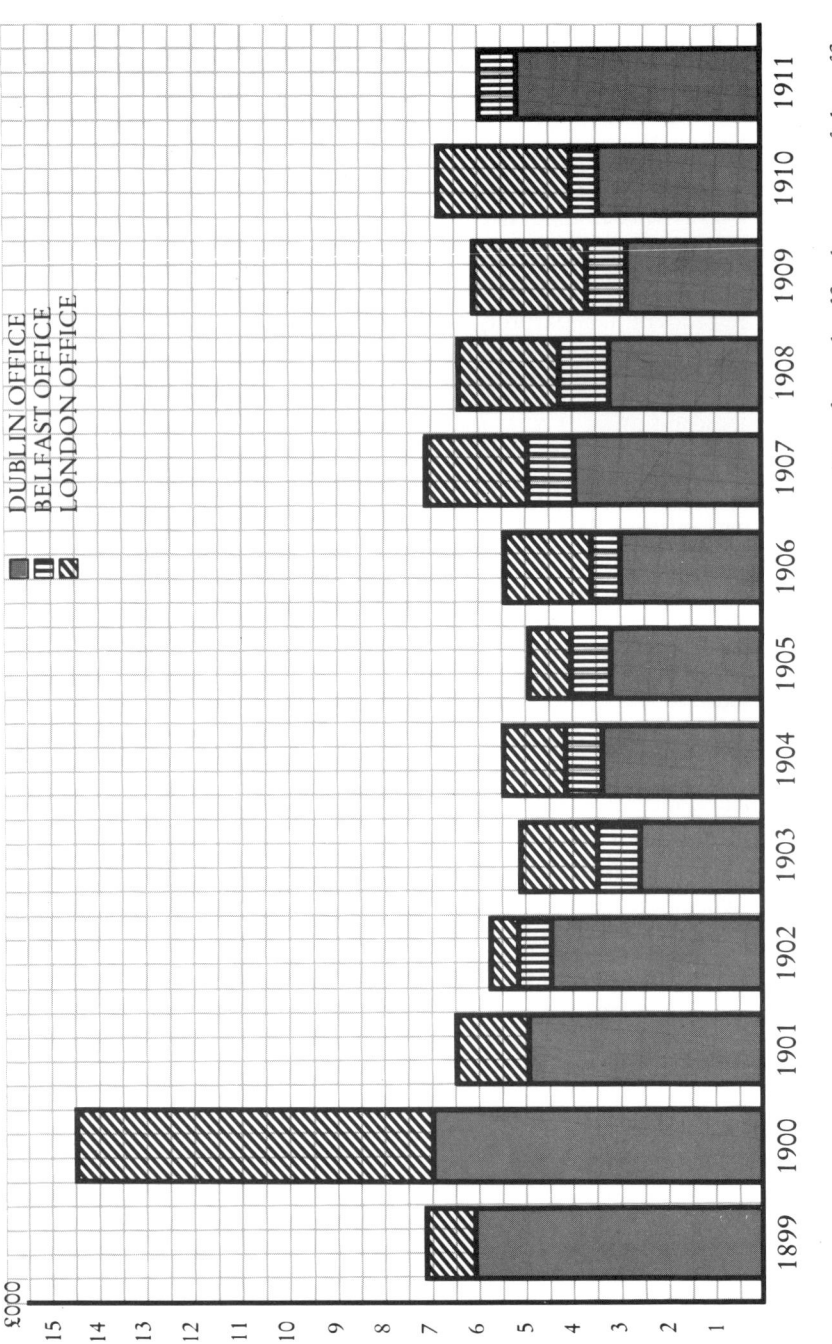

*Fees for each office less costs of that office

new partnership, called Craig Gardner and Harris, between Gardner, Harris and a David Allan of the London firm, who had qualified in Glasgow in 1902. By 1906 Harris was Chairman of the Carlton and the new Ritz hotels, and actively negotiating with the up-market Hamburg — America shipping line for the catering contract. Harris became a world-famous specialist in the management of hotels: it was said that he could tell whether or not a hotel was paying merely by looking at the laundry bill. His accountancy work, though no doubt meticulous, followed the practice of the day: in 1906 the *Irish Investors' Guardian*[23] commented approvingly on the Carlton Hotel's accounts (audited by David Allan), noting that they clearly didn't tell the whole truth — anyone capable of reading between the lines could see that there was probably a substantial hidden reserve being created. This was the best contemporary conservative style. Accountants were very conscious that less than half of registered companies survived ten years, and so the emphasis was on prudence, which meant, specifically, hidden reserves and low dividends. Twenty-five years later the Royal Mail case, and the imprisoning of Lord Kylsant for using these reserves to bolster profits and dividends, was to change this practice completely.

Gardner, representing the Dublin office, had a three-eighths profit share in the London firm, though as the deed put it, 'the said Robert Gardner shall not be obliged to attend to the business of the partnership any further than he shall think proper.' The London office, based at 20 Copthall Avenue (very near the headquarters of the English Institute) continued to remit profits to Dublin until 1910, by which time it was making more than Dublin and Belfast

---

[23] December 1906.

put together.[24] Clearly this relationship was not likely to last, and Harris bought out Craig Gardner in that year.

Soon the new firm of Harris, Allan and Co. had offices in Rangoon (a partner and four chartered accountants by 1913) and Hamburg, where they did all the accounting for the Hamburg-America line. Allan eventually left to set up Allan Charlesworth & Co., which among other accounts took over the audit of E. & J. Burke Ltd., Craig Gardner's largest audit client in the 1890s. The registration and secretarial work for the company was still done in the 1950s by Craig Gardner in Dublin. Later the audit was done jointly by the two firms.

In 1904, however, Craig Gardner's business was still firmly based in the three cities, with an overall turnover of just under £20,000 a year, of which about half came from Dublin. Both the London and Belfast offices were beginning to contribute nicely to profits, and the Dublin fee income, though it had dropped over the three previous years from a high of £15,598 in 1900 to £8,158 in 1903, had shown a slight recovery in 1904.

A new partnership deed had been signed in December 1903, giving Robert Gardner a one-half share in profits, Telford one-third and John Gardner one-sixth. (Like the order of names on a Chinese Politburo announcement, the changes in shares as the partnership deeds were renegotiated every five years show the partners recognising the respective contributions of each others' activity.) For the next few years fee income was static, averaging £9,300, a level which gave the two senior partners £2,700 and £1,800 respectively. The firm was well established in the popular mind: in 1908 the *Irish Investors' Guardian*, commenting on the annual report of the Dundalk & Newry Steampacket

---

[24] Profits remitted in 1910 were £2,692. Assuming this was three-eighths of total profits, the London firm was making a total profit of £7,200, and (on the 50 per cent rule) a fee income of £14,400. Dublin fee income for 1910 was £9,692. With a different set of personalities, Craig Gardner might well have become a London house with an Irish base, much as the centre of power in Thompson McLintock moved from Glasgow to London.

Co. Ltd wrote: 'Messrs Craig, Gardner & Co. are the auditors, which shows that the audit is no perfunctory one, as that eminent firm give a clear certificate in every respect to particularly full and detailed accounts'.[25] At another level, James Joyce, in *Ulysses*, has Bella Cohen, 'a massive whoremistress', exclaim in her best mannish tones (while sitting on Bloom's face): 'Guinness' preference shares are at sixteen three quarters. Curse me for a fool that I didn't buy that lot Craig and Gardner told me about. Just my infernal luck, curse it.'[26]

Perhaps the firm's security and comparative prosperity took the edge off the major partners' appetites, for they had both expanded their extra-curricular activities, as is described in the next chapter.

---

[25] Quoted in H.P. Smyth *The B. & I. Line* (Dublin 1984) p 145.
[26] James Joyce *Ulysses* Bodley Head ed (London 1960) p 646.

CHAPTER 4

WIDER HORIZONS
1904-24

After the turn of the century the atmosphere in the firm changed somewhat. The steady development of regular audit business in the 1890s meant that there was a firm basis for the existing income, and it was less necessary for the partners avidly to seek business. The firm was auditor to a third of the Irish commercial and industrial companies quoted on the Dublin Stock Exchange, representing 40 per cent of the issued capital of the sector. The nearest rival was Stokes Bros and Pim, with companies representing 29 per cent of the issued capital. Kean's, with four companies representing 7 per cent, was the third biggest firm. Craig Gardners were involved in the audit of two out of the nine banks, and seven out of nine large drapery concerns.[1]

This dominance of the drapery sector must have given the firm considerable planning problems, because virtually all the big stores had a year-end of 31 January, and they all prided themselves on getting the figures out quickly. Other big quoted companies such as Thom's the printers and Brooks, Thomas the builders merchants, had January year-ends, not to mention Johnston, Mooney and O'Brien, J.C. Parkes (metal merchants) and Thomas Dockrells with December year-ends.

Gardner maintained his prestige as the country's best-known accountant. In 1906, for instance, he was commissioned by the shareholders' committee of the National Assurance Company to investigate the company's affairs, which had gone badly wrong. In particular the shareholders wanted to know whether a Call of £6 per share on unpaid capital was justified. His report, which covered forty printed pages, was delivered less than a month after being commissioned. In summary he reported as follows.

The company's losses over the previous thirty-five years amounted to £343,500, chiefly in the Fire department, which

---

[1] Figures based on data in the *Irish Investors' Guardian* and the *Stock Exchange Intelligence* (1910); a few listed companies have been excluded from the reckoning as being British based.

had succeeded in losing money in Britain, in Canada, in the United States, and in France, Germany, Austria, Sweden, Africa, Argentina and Italy. The bulk of these losses occurred after the appointment of a Mr Cream as manager in 1896. Gardner pointed out that by 1900 the company was making misleading statements in its balance sheets — in one case the 'cash in hand and at bank' figure turned out to be a netted sum, concealing a Bank of Ireland overdraft of £23,000, against which was set various less tangible balances with overseas agents. In 1897 'a dividend was paid as the result of writing up the value of an unrealized asset' (the company's offices in College Green).

Around this time several of the directors and their families had begun to sell shares, keeping just enough to qualify as directors. As Gardner comments: 'at the time these shares were sold, the precarious position of the company was of course known to the directors.' Despite 'the absence of any proper records of existing risks', and the consequent 'impossibility of obtaining even an approximate estimate of all the liabilities', it was clear that the £6 Call was the very least the shareholders could expect.

The graph of Craig Gardner's fee income shows a marked damping around this time, with the peaks and troughs that it had previously displayed virtually disappearing. Age no doubt had something to do with this. Robert Gardner, for thirty years the firm's main business-getter, was now in his sixties, and was becoming involved in other matters. David Telford was director of two railway companies and two other companies as well as being Chairman of the Dublin Theatre Company. A growing recognition of the status and usefulness of chartered accountants was leading to interesting invitations for the partners to sit on boards and committees. Traditionally it had been the bank official whose duty it was 'to play a prominent role by holding office in clubs and societies (a banker was almost invariably treasurer)';[2] it is a measure of the social development of the accountancy profession in the twentieth century that accountants are now invariably the first choice

1891-1919 DUBLIN FEES & PARTNERS % OF FEES

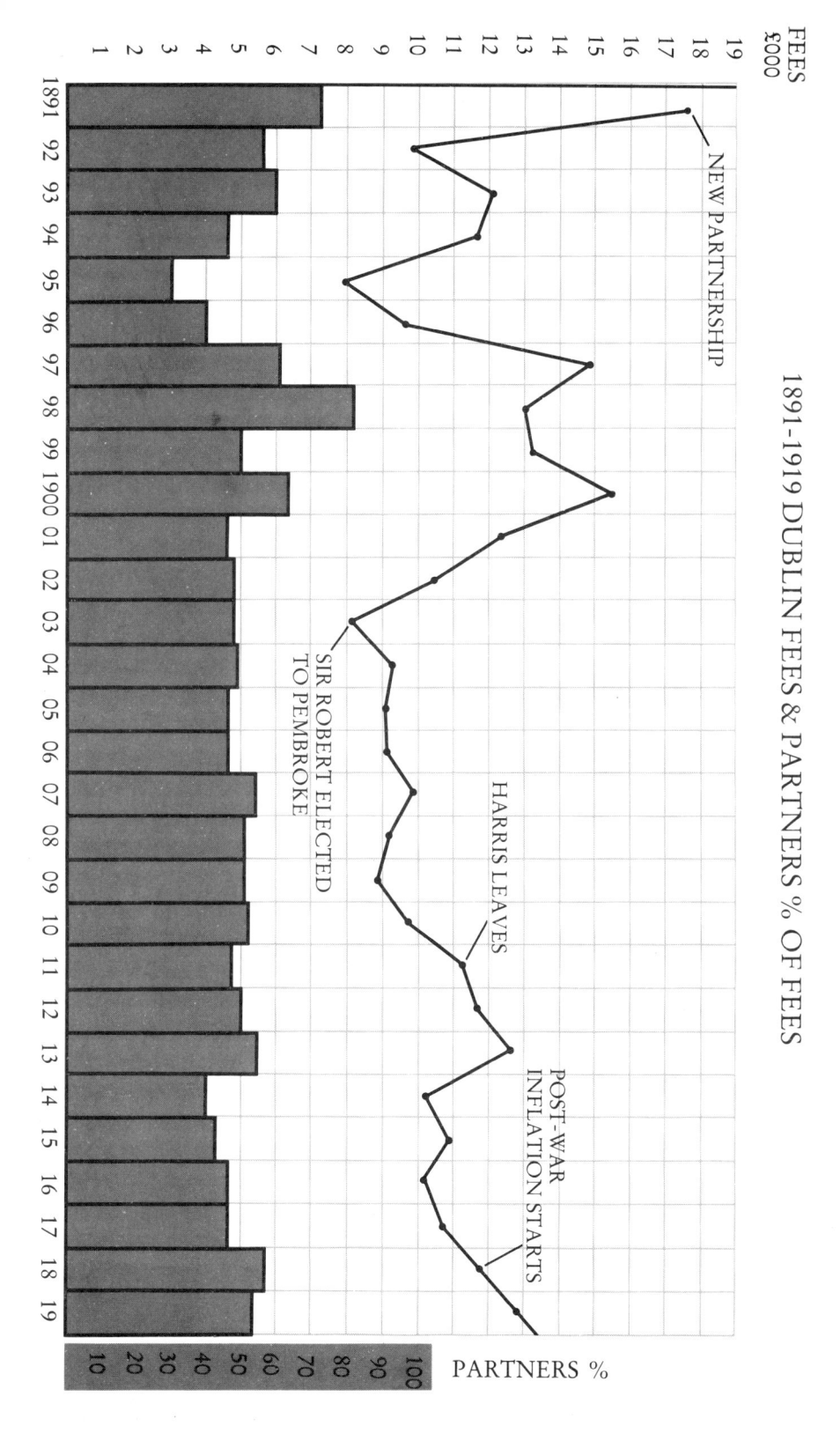

for this and many other financial responsibilities. The third partner, after William Harris's departure, was John Gardner, Robert's son, who never found the profession congenial.

At the level below partner, there was some investment in staff during the period from 1903, for the ratio of salaries to fees regularly went over the 50 per cent level for the first time. In 1910, George Hill Tulloch, a Scots Presbyterian, who had joined the firm from Turquand, Young in 1904, was made a partner. Tulloch was one of the first of the influx of Scottish accountants that were later to become a feature of the firm. Ireland was an attractive destination for the Scots accountants at this time, for the starting salary was considerably higher than was paid in Scotland and, because a Scottish principal was allowed to employ more articled clerks than the two allowed to English or Irish accountants, there was a ready supply. At the same time Scotland had a reputation for providing hard-headed managers and financial men. Tulloch's original share of the profits was one-tenth, with a salary of £300.

Gardner and the Pembroke Council

At this time Dublin city council's writ ran only to the canals; beyond, notably in Rathmines and Pembroke, were self-governing townships (since the Local Government Act 1898 technically urban district councils). In 1901 Robert Gardner was asked by certain ratepayers living in the Pembroke area to stand for the council.[3] The finances of

---

[2] F.S.L. Lyons 'Reflections on a Bicentenary' in *Bicentenary Essays, Bank of Ireland 1783-1983* (Dublin 1983) p 200.
[3] Unless otherwise specified, details of Gardner's activities on the Council are taken from the Minutes of the Pembroke Township, which are held in the Dublin City Archives.

the township had been in disarray for some time, and he was part of a ratepayers' revolt to try to put things in order, and to reduce rates. The Council had for years depended on the Earl of Pembroke and various rich residents to help them out if they got into difficulties, and this had resulted in extravagant and ill-managed systems. Gardner was elected to the Pembroke council in January 1902. Only two members of the old council were re-elected.

When the new council looked at the books, things were much worse than expected. Two views quickly made themselves clear. The nationalists formed a steady voting block who wanted rates reduced, and would not be sorry to see the council absorbed by Dublin City. The addition of Rathmines and Pembroke to the city rates would have increased the sorely pressed city's income by a third. Since virtually all the inhabitants of the two townships worked in the city, there was some logic in the absorption idea — from the nationalist point of view, also, the existence of these largely unionist enclaves just outside the city must have been galling. The other side, led by Gardner, assumed that the survival of the district was desirable, and could be achieved mainly by strong management.

Gardner examined the books and decided that the excess of liabilities over assets was £14,000. Michael Crowley[4] the Catholic accountant was brought in by the chairman (who was supported by the nationalists) and estimated the deficit at £20,657. The difference between the two figures rested on whether money in a special (No. 2) bank acount could be used for general purposes. Gardner, in his typically robust way, assumed it could. After much argument a three-year plan was proposed by Gardner and his allies, in which the

[4] Born 1849, educated Christian Brothers and privately, member of the Chartered Accountants of Ontario in 1885, signatory of the Irish Charter. Fellow of the Royal Statistical Society and author of *Directory and Statistics of Limited Liability Companies registered in Ireland* (Dublin 1901) and other books. Uncle of Vincent Crowley, who founded Kennedy, Crowley which later amalgamated with Stokes Brothers and Pim to become Stokes Kennedy Crowley.

rates would be doubled. This was of course far from what the new council had been elected to do.

On 6 May, at a meeting to agree a new rate of 12s 9d in the £, the chairman, in an attempt to block the proceedings, read out a further statement of account drafted by Michael Crowley, which (as *The Irish Times* put it) 'showed the deficiency of liabilities and assets of £37,000. Mr Gardner said the figures were nonsense, and attached an adjective to the word. The chairman said he had the figures before him, and went into several items at length, making the liabilities even more. Mr Gardner said that the Chairman could not shove that down their throats. The accountant referred to had before certified the amount to be considerably less.' It eventually appeared that Michael Crowley had included in the new estimate a sum of £16,000, being the whole of a mortgage on which the council, in its difficulties, had defaulted on a single payment. The issue boiled down to the technical one of valuation. Gardner subsequently 'withdrew the adjective, but not the word'.

At this point one of the councillors, James McCann, a stockbroker and recently elected nationalist MP for the Stephen's Green division, resigned in protest against the new rate, an occasion not much regretted by Gardner. 'Mr Gardner said he was sorry Mr McCann was leaving, but when asked repeatedly to give his views on the financial state of the township, he had invariably replied "I have no suggestion to make" and he (Mr Gardner) failed to see the value of that criticism to the township.'[5]

Later in May Gardner proposed a motion to the council in favour of presenting an address to Edward VII on the occasion of the coronation. Some time before, the council had presented a similar address, via a local priest, to Leo XIII on his twenty-fifth anniversary in the papacy. This did nothing to mollify two Catholic members of the council,

[5] *The Irish Times* 13 May 1902.

who objected strongly to Gardner's proposal. One of them, Mr Kennedy, was reported as objecting particularly to the coronation oath: 'I must protest against this. As a Catholic I feel with millions of His Majesty's subjects that we have been grossly outraged by this objectionable oath, and by being branded as idolators, in other words, that we worship sticks and stones and marble and such things. I also object to it on political grounds. I object on account of having two-thirds of the country under coercion at the moment, and some of our best and truest men buried in prison dens.'[6] The motion was passed however, and a subcommittee headed by Gardner deputed to put the idea into action. Later that week Gardner attended a large meeting of the Citizens Coronation Committee, which was to consider suitable ways of commemorating the great event.

The rows in the council didn't stop there. In September both Gardner and the chairman resigned, and Gardner was asked to accept the chairmanship, which he did, on condition he was also made chairman of the finance committee. Three days later payments from the hitherto blocked No. 2 account started. By January 1903 the crisis was under control, and the finance committee went back to meeting monthly. Perhaps feeling his job was done, and like so many of the city's grandees finding political life uncongenial, Gardner again resigned in March 1903, but was persuaded to return 'to carry out his promises in respect of the finances of the council.' The new rate was 10s in the £. Monthly income and expenditure accounts began to be presented to the meetings of the council for the first time (though without cumulative figures, or variance against forecast), and the rate steadily reduced to 9s 3d in 1908. By this time the council was financially strong enough to acquire land, the plot between Herbert Park and Morehampton Road, and to take an active part

---

[6] *The Irish Times* 24 May 1902.

A view of the 1907 Exhibition grounds in Herbert Park. The accounts of the Exhibition prepared by Craig Gardner showed a loss of £100,083 over its five months' duration.

in the Irish International Exhibition of May 1907, which was held in Herbert Park.7

In the meantime Robert Gardner had been knighted, one of the two Irish knights in the birthday honours list of 30 June 1905. *The Irish Times* commented:

> Mr Gardner is a member of an eminent firm of chartered accountants, is very prominent as Chairman of Pembroke Town Council, and has done excellent work in promoting the erection of artisan's dwellings in the city of Dublin and of ameliorating generally the lot of the working classes.

Gardner was re-elected to the council in 1908, once again heading the poll. In May the following year, however, Gardner resigned again, and this time he stuck to his resolution. The finances of the Pembroke Council had been put on a reasonable footing, a fact that enabled the council to resist the sporadic attempts of the city corporation to annex the township for another twenty years.

Telford and Dublin Theatre

David Telford, the other principal partner, was equally deeply involved in activities outside the firm. In 1897 he was approached to be Chairman of a syndicate set up to

---

7 The Dublin United Tramway Company (a Craig Gardner client) guaranteed £12,500 towards the Exhibition's expenses in 1904, a transaction that caused some comment in the *Irish Investors' Guardian*, though the paper reluctantly concluded that there was some business justification, since the Tramway Company could hope for an extra £56,000 in fares as a result of the Exhibition.

acquire the Theatre Royal (a variety theatre in Hawkins Street, where Hawkins House now is) from the estate of Michael Gunn. In 1907 the company acquired the Gaiety Theatre from Mrs Gunn, and so had two out of the three commercial theatres in Dublin. Both theatres depended very largely on touring companies from London, whom they exposed to what one critic acidly described as

> a very large audience, composed of the intensely uncritical and ignorant type only too common in Dublin — that they should be noisy and ill-behaved is nothing ... but that they should scream with boorish laughter when one of the characters spoke a few words of Irish is scarcely to be credited.[8]

In 1904 the Theatre Royal joined with the other theatres in opposing the licence for the new Abbey Theatre. In the end the licence was granted, but subject to the restriction that they could only show:

> plays in the Irish or English language written by Irish writers on Irish subjects, or such dramatic works as would tend to interest the public in the higher works of dramatic art.

Obviously, these areas were not felt to be a commercial threat. A few years later, having seen what the Abbey was about, the companies withdrew their objection. At what was described as 'a glittering social gathering', in October 1910, called to discuss the affairs of the Irish Literary Theatre,

---

[8] Frank Fay, quoted in R. Hogan *The Modern Irish Drama* vol. 1 (Dublin 1975).

Lady Gregory announced that Mr Telford had promised on behalf of the other theatres in Dublin, that they would not oppose the renewal of the licence of the Abbey Theatre. This was, perhaps, the best subscription that they had received.[9]

The general Dublin audience's taste in theatre didn't much improve in the next few years, and touring companies became harder to entice to Dublin. At an enquiry in 1913 Telford defended his company's offerings. He identified 'a change in the public taste to light opera, musical comedy, and variety entertainment. In self-defence many of the best theatrical people have had to follow their patrons to the music halls . . . it's entirely a question of supply and demand. I am continually being told — by the best people, too — how much they appreciate the short, bright Hippodrome entertainments at present running at the Royal.'[10] The Hippodrome was a kind of circus, exemplified by acts such as: 'De Gracia's Assam Elephants, so well remembered in their cricket match'.

Later that year Telford put his foot down about allowing Madame Markievicz to take part in a play in the Gaiety. In a letter from Trinity Chambers, he wrote: 'Owing to the high feeling which prevails in the city at the moment, and owing to the prominent part which the Countess has taken in the labour disputes, I honestly do not think that her appearance on the stage would be good for business . . .'

As well as his directorships, Telford also described himself, in a contemporary 'Who's who' as 'interested in farming, and spends as much time as he can afford at his country residence in co. Antrim.' It is curious to see the *fin de siècle* anti-materialism that partly motivated the nationalist

---

[9] *The Irish Times* quoted in R. Hogan *The Modern Irish Drama* vol. 4 (Dublin 1979).
[10] R. Hogan *The Modern Irish Drama* vol. 4 (Dublin 1979) pp 290-291.

movement receiving expression in this way. In fact this rural myth, that business, though of course necessary, was an interruption to the real life which was related to the unchanging agricultural rhythms of the countryside, was very common in British urban thinking in the late nineteenth and early twentieth centuries. It was a civilised view, but not one that led to the devoted pursuit of business growth. The fact that there seems to have been very little of the countryman about Telford, who was a toughminded, straightforward, urban businessman, merely demonstrated how strong the myth was.[11]

The Great War and After, 1914-1924

At the outbreak of war in 1914, many Irish accountants joined up. David Telford, who served as President of the Institute in 1915/16 and 1916/17, reported that by the middle of the war 82 members and their clerks had joined up. In the end 114 Members and Assistants joined up, of which 70 were from Belfast (in 1914 exactly half of the Members worked in the North of Ireland). Robert Gardner's son was already in the 21st Lancers, and others immediately joined from Craig Gardner's, including E. Telford, a son of David's, who had recently qualified. He joined the Connaught Rangers, and was eventually killed. In all, seventeen Craig Gardner men joined up, of whom ten never reappeared on the Institute's lists of members, and so may be presumed (at least the majority of them) to have died.

A few members of the staff were involved in nationalist politics. The most famous of these was Michael Collins,

---

[11] E. MacDowel Cosgrave (ed.) *Pike's Contemporary Biographies: Dublin and Co. Dublin in the Twentieth Century* (Brighton and London 1908).

who came from London in 1916 to be in Dublin for the Rising. He spent most of the few months he was in the firm working in Boileau and Boyd, the druggists, which had been a monthly job since the 1890s. Joseph McGrath, who was later Minister for Industry and Commerce, and Chairman of the Irish Hospital Sweepstakes, and his brother George McGrath were also in the firm at the same time. Dr Robinson describes an interview he had with Joe McGrath:

> He recalled how George McGrath, his brother, was employed by Craig Gardners from 1910 to 1918 and spent a considerable part of the early years working on liquidations in Sligo and in Tuam, and was actually working in Tuam when he got married. George arranged for his brother Joseph to be employed by Craig Gardners in the autumn of 1915 and Joseph was almost immediately sent by Sir Robert Gardner to conduct a liquidation in Newbridge, where he spent most of the six months during which he was employed by the firm. He recollects Sir Robert arriving in the snow in a hackney, dressed in a fur-lined coat and top hat and inspecting the premises in a sprightly manner.
>   Joseph McGrath returned to Dublin on the eve of St. Patrick's Day, 1916, and was there to participate in the rising some five weeks later.[12] After the rising he was on the run, and Sir Robert, who had lost a son at Suvla Bay, was apparently sympathetically inclined and told George McGrath that when Joseph returned to Dublin he was to come back into the firm. David Telford, however, warned George McGrath that Joseph needn't return as he would not have him . . .

---

[12] McGrath was in action in Marrowbone Lane in Dublin, and was later imprisoned in Wormwood Scrubbs and Brixton.

The only other member of Craig Gardners who was concerned in the Movement was Joseph Considine, a copyist, and something of a poet, whose brother had participated in the 1916 rising but who had, himself, taken no part until the Anglo-Irish struggle in 1919/21. Considine, apparently, was a great favourite of George Tulloch's, one of the partners in Craig Gardners, from whom he used to draw his salary considerably in advance, and Joseph McGrath thinks it likely that Considine may have used Tulloch's room for meetings during the troubles (as was the tradition in the firm) and have beeen helped by Tulloch while interned. This would seem to be in character.[13]

The McGrath connection was later to be immensely helpful to the firm, through the Irish Hospital Sweepstake, one of the mainstays of income during and after the 1930s and later the connection brought Waterford Glass to the firm as a client from its beginning after the Second World War. In 1918 George McGrath became accountant to the national movement on Collins' request, being given the task of looking after the National Loan and the national accounts. He later became the first Comptroller and Auditor General.

The Great War was good for the Irish economy, particularly in the north. The development of the audit component of business meant that the firm increasingly benefited from growth in the economy, rather than doing best in bad periods through insolvency business. In Dublin the outbreak of war apparently interrupted a growth period, for fees had risen 30 per cent between 1910 and 1913, and then fell back to an average of £10,000 per annum

---

[13] H. Robinson *A History of Accountants in Ireland* 2nd edn (Dublin 1983) pp 113-14.

in 1914-17. Accountants found they were called on to perform an increased range of duties. Income tax was raised to unprecedented heights, making it increasingly worthwhile to hire a professional. As the war dragged on, the government tried to prevent profiteering by imposing Excess Profits Duty, and by controlling firms' costs.

In Ireland another source of work came from the national situation, as accountants were asked to certify for compensation damage suffered by firms. After the Easter Rising, for instance, Craig Gardner's certified the damage to Arnott's caused by the fighting and the loss by looting. Another side-effect of the Rising was the acquisition of the Eason audit. Eason's historian described how this occurred:

> The accounts of Eason's had always been audited internally. Hallet, the accountant, was auditor . . . until June 1901, when the new Companies Act prohibited servants of the company acting as auditors. George Herbert Carpenter of the National Museum, who became professor in the College of Science in 1904, was appointed auditor. In fact he continued to be auditor until 1917. At this point the directors reported to the general meeting of 1917: 'The destruction of the premises and stock in April 1916 raised so many difficult questions in the preparation of the Balance Sheet that Mr G.H. Carpenter informed the directors that he felt unable to undertake this work any longer.' The work was entrusted to G.H. Tulloch of Craig Gardner & Co. It was characteristically still a family arrangement. George Hill Tulloch was married to the widow of William Waugh Eason. The audit was entrusted to him in a personal capacity rather than as a partner in Craig Gardner & Co., and his reports even had a slight tone of business conversation within a family circle. The introduction of professional auditing was . . . the occasion for the

first time of serious attempts to estimate net profits at a departmental level.[14]

At this time Eason's was one of the largest companies in the city, employing nearly seven hundred people, and making considerable profits. The company's management accounting system was still rudimentary: 'until 1909 there had been no attempt to separate the cost of sales of stationery goods purchased from outside suppliers and those manufactured in the firm's own factory in Gloucester Street, and in fact there was no method of deducing whether the factory itself operated at a profit or at a loss.' The lack of sophisticated overhead cost allocation and other accounting controls must have been common at this time, for the Eason family were highly numerate.

The only direct involvement the firm had with the Troubles was in June 1922, at the very beginning of the civil war. Republicans who objected to the Anglo-Irish Treaty, which had been signed the previous December, had taken over the Four Courts in April, and on 27 June had kidnapped the pro-treaty General O'Connell, Deputy Chief of Staff of the National Army. The government despatched an ultimatum demanding surrender to the Four Courts at 3.40 pm on 28 June, and shelling started an hour later.

At 3.30 pm a delivery van pulled up to Craig Gardner's offices in Trinity Street and began unloading stores of bread, sugar and tea. As the parcels were carried through the door the cashier, Tom Scott, reported the matter to George Tulloch. Tulloch remonstrated with a man standing inside the door, saying that there seemed to be some mistake. The man showed a revolver and said that there was no mistake. Shortly afterwards several armed men, some with revolvers and some with rifles, came into the

[14] L. M. Cullen *History of Easons* (Dublin 1988).

office. They gave staff a few minutes to clear their desks and leave.[15] After the occupation it was found that one line of windows on the first, second and third floors had been smashed, apparently by Free State rifle fire directed from the Bank of Ireland. The rooms were littered with broken glass and plaster, and bread, butter and bully beef had been trampled into the carpets. A skylight in the attic had been torn off its hinges and one of the lavatory doors, which had been locked, was prised open and the lavatory damaged. The firm lodged a claim for malicious damages, and subsequently received a refund of £42 11s 3d. This included two raincoats taken, and damage to ledgers belonging to Kings Hospital and W. & P. Thompson Ltd.

In 1917 Sir Robert, then aged nearly eighty, decided to retire, and a deed of dissolution of the partnership was signed, giving him an entitlement to 40 per cent of the profits after payment of the remaining partners' salaries for the next five years, reducing to 32 per cent (40 per cent of four-fifths) thereafter. A new partnership agreement, to continue until the death of Robert Gardner, was signed by Telford, Tulloch and John Gardner, giving them profit shares of 45 per cent, 30 per cent and 25 per cent respectively. Three years later, on 24 November 1920, Sir Robert died at his home in Clyde Road. *The Irish Times'* obituary noted that he 'was auditor of many important companies, including the National Bank. As Chairman of the Pembroke Council he rendered very valuable services in placing the affairs of the Council on a sound business basis. He was an excellent administrator, and was very popular with the members of the Council.'[16] In January the following year a new partnership deed was signed, this time bringing Edward Buckley from Belfast into the main agreement. The new partners, with their share of profits, were David Telford (35 per cent), George Hill Tulloch

---

[15] Their object, apparently, was to cover Jury's Hotel.
[16] *The Irish Times* 25 November 1920.

(30 per cent), Edward Buckley (25 per cent) and John Gardner (10 per cent).

The long-term survival of the firm was now a serious question. The two senior partners, Telford and Tulloch, were in their late sixties and late forties respectively; John Gardner was in his late fifties, and his share in the profits was nearly as low as it had been when he was first made a partner thirty years before. The purchasing power (at 1914 prices) of the firm's income was less than it had been in 1910, though the rapid increase in cash fees since the end of the war may have concealed this fact from those not used to thinking in inflationary terms. The firm had no qualified Associates as potential new partners.

In an attempt to hold on to their senior men, a staff bonus scheme had been set up in 1918. The scheme arranged for part of the profits to be credited to the names of the principal staff members. The partners decided year by year how much should be allocated, and to whom. The amount credited was to bear interest at 5 per cent, added to the capital, which was paid to the widow in the event of death. If the employee left the firm, he would be paid the amount standing to his credit, unless he set up business, or took employment, as an accountant in Dublin or within 60 miles thereof. By 1924 £3,000 of profits had been added to the scheme, five per cent of the total partners' receipts over the six years. Credits stood in the names of J. Donnelly, E.J. Shott, G.H. Hill, G. McGrath and a dozen others.

In 1922 a row blew up which underlined the firm's precarious position. The sole surviving record is a letter sent to John Gardner by his three partners, which is marked 'rec'd on return from Limerick 2 March 22.'

Trinity Chambers,
40 & 41 Dame Street,
Dublin.

Sir,
You have already been informed that you, being a member of the co-partnership of Craig Gardner & Company, Accountants of Trinity Chambers Dublin and 53, Donegall Place Belfast, under an indenture dated the 5th day of January 1921 made between the undersigned David Telford of the first part, the undersigned George Hill Tulloch of the second part, the undersigned Edward Buckley of the third part, and you the said John Gardner of the fourth part, have been guilty of conduct which in the opinion of us and each of us has been detrimental to the business of the said partnership; said conduct consisted of gross negligence and other acts on your part when auditing the books accounts and documents of certain clients of the firm. Now we, the undersigned co-partners, hereby give you notice that for the reasons above mentioned, on the 31st day of March 1922, the said partnership will be put an end to, so far as you are concerned, and that from said 31st day of March 1922 you shall be excluded from said partnership . . . as witness our hands this 27th day of February 1922.

(signed) D.Telford, G.H.Tulloch, Edw.Buckley

To/
John Gardner Esq.
1 Morehampton Road
Dublin.

It is difficult to imagine a more explicit and categorical statement, and one from which little or no appeal would lie. And yet the private ledger (still, as it had been since 1890, in David Telford's hand, which was now becoming a little shaky) records that John Gardner continued to receive his 10 per cent share for the next two years amounting to nearly £3,000.

Amalgamation

Without qualified younger men the future of the firm was doubtful, and it was not clear where they were to come from. In the profession as a whole in Ireland there were forty-two Fellows of the Institute, and sixty-four Associates.[17] In Dublin there were thirteen Fellows and nineteen Associates, of which Craig Gardner had three Fellows, Stokes Brothers and Pim three Fellows and John Mackie & Co., a relatively new firm, two Fellows and two Associates. M. Crowley & Co. had one Fellow and three Associates. If an amalgamation was sought, Stokes were the firm most like Craig Gardner, an old established firm, whose second generation, both of Stokes and Pims, had recently entered partnership.

The other sizeable Protestant firm, John Mackie and Co., were more interesting. The senior partner, Mackie, was an ardent liberal, a Home Ruler, interested in proportional representation and in the informational aspect of accounts. The next partner, Gabriel Brock, was clearly brilliant: he had been awarded a special prize by the Institute for his marks in the Intermediate examination in 1910. He was to become the leading accountant of his day. Brock's father was Scottish, and an agent to landowners in Drogheda; Brock had started his education at a Christian Brothers' school before being transferred to St. Andrews. John Russell, a Scottish Presbyterian, had been a partner since 1917, and was eventually to become senior partner of Craig Gardner in 1954. None of the three was over 50, and Brock

---

[17] By contrast there were at this time 135 members of the Stock Exchange in Ireland, including 85 based in Dublin.

was not yet 40. Telford had his eye particularly on Brock, and after an assiduous wooing on his part, the two firms amalgamated in 1924.

The new firm started with seven partners. John Gardner was out, so there were the three remaining Craig Gardner partners (Telford, Tulloch and Buckley), and three Mackie partners (Mackie, Brock and Russell). A new Craig Gardner partner, Eustace Shott, was also admitted, thus preserving the Craig Gardner voting majority. Shott, whose father was a mine manager in Wales, had come to the firm before the war. He joined up in 1914, and achieved the rank of Captain. After the war he returned to Craig Gardner, took articles and qualified in 1923.

In the new arrangement Telford was paid a fixed sum of £2,000, and of the remaining profits Tulloch got 25 per cent, Buckley 24 per cent, Mackie 18 per cent, Brock 13 per cent and Russell and Shott 10 per cent each. The firm was now convincingly the largest in Dublin, with five out of thirteen Fellows and three Associates, one of whom was David Telford's son David who, after an adventurous war flying planes from Bristol to northern France, had recently qualified.

Among the competition was a new firm — Gardner, Donnelly & Co. — a breakaway from Craig Gardner, which consisted of John Gardner and John Donnelly. Donnelly had been one of the firm's senior men, manager of the income tax department. Gardner, Donnelly continued to do some audit work in partnership with Craig Gardner, for instance of the match manufacturer Paterson's of which Telford was a director, but it was not an amicable split. Telford refused to pay the £476 of staff bonus that Donnelly had accumulated, and the matter went to law. It was eventually settled out of court. John Gardner died in 1926, and John Donnelly in 1938, and the business was for some years carried on by his widow in conjunction with Kevans & Co.

CHAPTER 5

AMALGAMATION WITH MACKIE'S 1924-29

The amalgamation with John Mackie & Co. in 1924 was the most significant development of the firm since the split between Craig and Gardner in 1875. The ethos of the firm changed in a way that had not occurred on the promotion of Telford and his colleagues in 1890, since they had been after all already part of Craig Gardner. The new partners, especially Mackie and Brock, also brought a technical brilliance and a breadth of view to the firm.

Mackie, who was born in 1876, was active as a Home Ruler, a liberal, and a proponent of proportional representation. He had been a prime mover in the Dublin Accountants Students Society in 1908, a society which combined members from chartered and incorporated societies. He was Honorary Secretary to the Institute in 1919/20. He had taken Brock as his partner in 1913, when the latter was only twenty-seven. Brock had had some difficulties getting accepted by the Institute, firstly because his name had been incorrectly spelt on his Intermediate certificate, and secondly because his principal was based in London rather than Dublin; after some litigation the point was cleared up. The third partner, John Russell, had joined the firm in 1917 from Scotland.

John Mackie & Co.'s total fees for the year before the amalgamation were £7,527, of which nearly 20 per cent came from their London office, which appears to have been largely run by Mackie himself. Craig Gardner's fees for the year ended March 1923 were Dublin £16,563, Belfast £8,443. The new partnership therefore had a total turnover of £32,000, of which the three Mackie partners contributed a quarter, and received a combined share of 41 per cent of the profits (after salaries). The firm employed five articled clerks who came into Craig Gardner's with the firm, T. Neary, L. Davies, J. Harris, W. Crawford and C. McReadie; there were also twelve or thirteen unqualified clerks. After qualifying, Crawford was to serve as Secretary of the Institute from 1934 to 1955, and Secretary of the Irish Banks' Joint Committee from 1942.

For some time after the merger the two firms continued as separate entities, with John Mackie & Co. in Nassau Street and Craig Gardner in Dame Street. Various schemes were discussed with a view to uniting the two firms physically. One idea suggested was to take a floor or two in the old Jury's Hotel, where a number of Inspectors of Taxes were situated, having been burned out of the Custom House. However by August 1924 it was decided to take a lease of No. 39 Dame Street, and break through a door to Nos 40 and 41 on the first floor level.

John Mackie drew up a meticulous memorandum discussing the implications of the proposed move, and making various suggestions for the new combined office. From the first sentence, which declares, no doubt with political intent, that the two older Craig Gardner partners, Telford and Tulloch, should be put to the minimum of inconvenience during the move, this document gives a vivid insight into the internal conditions and daily workings of the firm. It also provides a snapshot of the slowly developing office practice of the time; note for instance the suggestion (see page 117), that flat-top rather than sloping 'stand-up' desks should now be provided for all. By implication, the memo also provides an insight into the practical difficulties of combining two firms in an era when operations were both on a smaller scale and also very much more personally run than nowadays. In many details, both small and large, the ordinary house rules were different in the two firms, from the payment of national health contributions (Mackie's paid the employees' share, Craig Gardner's did not) to the provision of statistical information on time spent on audits. The memorandum is therefore worth quoting at length (omissions of ephemeral matter are indicated by . . .).[1]

---

[1] Part of the memo dealt with details of office restructuring and allocation, and these materials make up Appendix 3.

Memorandum on the Proposed Concentration of the Businesses of Craig Gardner & Co. and John Mackie and Co. at 39, 40 & 41 Dame Street, Dublin.

This memorandum is based on the following assumptions:

(1) That Mr. Telford and Mr. Tullock[2] should be put to the minimum of inconvenience.

(2) That the detail work in connection with Mr. Telford's Department should be distributed amongst his colleagues.

(3) That the business should be departmentalised with a view to spreading the responsibility for the allocation of the work, the control of staff, the arrangements for holidays, etc.

(4) That a complete register should be kept of all papers, etc. inwards and outwards.

(5) That all time, except in the case of Mr. Telford and the cashier's department, should be fully accounted for, analysed, summarised and posted monthly.

(6) That a separate section should be provided for each Client's papers, and that there should be ready access to such sections by reference to an alphabetical register in the Cashier's Office.

(7) That the arrangement and equipment of the Clerks' offices should be designed with a view to promoting the comfort of the Staff and, accordingly, facilitating the rapid and efficient despatch of the work.

---

[2] This typist's error was later corrected in pen.

(8) That full advantage should be taken of such mechanical devices as the Underwood 18″ Typewriter; public and private telephones; the Comptometer; the Addressing Machine; the Tickler;[3] the Card Index, etc.

(9) That access to the rooms in No. 39 Dame Street will be given in October.

(10) That the transfer from No. 30 Nassau Street will be completed not later than 30th November, i.e. the whole Dublin business will be concentrated in Dame Street five or six weeks before the 'busy season' commences next January.

Equipment of Rooms:

(1) The existing equipment in Dame Street and Nassau Street should, of course, be utilised as far as possible, but much of it is entirely unsuitable and should be disposed of as the most is not being made of the available floor space.

(2) The head of each Department should have sufficient lock-up accommodation to enable all the current papers of the Clients in his Department to be filed in his room on the basis of providing each Client with a section large enough to take:

(1) the office copies of Accounts for (say) 3 years;
(2) a foolscap file for copies of the Firm's Reports to the Client;
(3) a foolscap file for correspondence with the Client;

---

[3] A card index system.

(4) a foolscap file for correspondence with the Inland Revenue Authorities;[4]
(5) a foolscap size Private Ledger.

(NOTE: The Accounts in (1) and the papers in (2), (3) and (4) above should not be tied up or fastened together, but left loose on proper date order so that they may be referred to without inconvenience and consequent loss of time.)

(3) The tables at present used by the Typists should, where suitable, be transferred to the Partners' rooms or made available for some of the Senior Assistants, and the Typists should be supplied with tables of a uniform type, and with comfortable chairs.
The tables should be capable of holding:
(1) an 18" Underwood Machine;
(2) a nest of 'clip-on' drawers for stationery, etc, &
(3) a letter tray.

(4) With the object of enabling the Typists to take off the required copies of Accounts for Clients and the Revenue at one operation, it is suggested that all the Typists should be supplied with 18" Underwood Machines.

(5) All the Senior Assistants and most of the others should be provided with separate flat top tables. The additional tables required might be made on the lines

---

[4] The Revenue Commissioners Order, 1923, made by the Executive Council in February of that year, rendered this usage somewhat out of date.

of those in use in the Offices of Inspectors of Taxes.[5]

(6) The Cashier's Office should be supplied with suitable Filing Cabinets for Time Records, Clients' Accounts, etc., and a Filing Table with screwed-down sections to facilitate the sorting of the carbon copies of letters, etc. by Departments.

(NOTE: The Loose Leaf System could be extended to Mr. Telford's Department without interfering with his use of a copying Letter Book, by arranging that carbon copies of Mr. Telford's letters shall be made in addition to the press copies.)[6]

(7) Each of the Clerks' rooms should be provided with:
(1) a press containing a section for each Clerk, with sections for Stationery, etc
(2) a sufficient number of chairs;
(3) a Brief Stand for the temporary accommodation of books, etc.

(8) Mr. Wright should be provided with an Addressograph, an Addressall, or other suitable machine so as to obviate the embarrassing demands which are made upon the Staff outside his department in connection with the preparation of Dividend Warrants, etc.

(9) The Waiting Room (1) should have a good table and six or eight chairs.

---

[5] The older furniture was mostly sloping 'stand up' writing desks. One of them was kept in the Cashier's office until the move to Ballsbridge in 1968.
[6] Telford obviously preferred to stick to the very old-fashioned letter-book; his letters would have been typed with a purple inked ribbon, put into a book with tissue paper leaves and a damp cloth and put under a press to make a copy.

(10) The Board Room (16) should be furnished with a large table; about eighteen chairs; coat & hat racks; an umbrella stand and a brief stand for the Secretary's papers.

CONDITIONS OF SERVICE:

Hours and Luncheon Intervals:

Hours: Monday to Friday — 9.30 to 5.30
Saturdays — 9.30 to 1.30

Luncheon Interval: Monday to Friday — 1 hour

Members of the Female Staff who go home for lunch and require an extra ¼ hour will require to attend at 9.15 a.m.

(The Nassau Street hours are 9 to 5, and on Saturdays 9 to 1, with 1½ hours luncheon intervals for the Female Staff and 1 hour for the Male Staff.)

Holidays:

Under 5 years' service: 14 working days, including 3 Saturdays.

Over 5 years' continuous service: 1 extra working day for each additional year of continuous service up to a maximum of 19 working days, including 4 Saturdays.

(In Nassau Street the holidays extend from Friday night until the morning of the following Tuesday fortnight, i.e. 14 working days, including 3 Saturdays, and the Holiday List is generally made up early in May, so that the Staff have ample notice of the holiday arrangements.)

Overtime:

While every effort will be made to keep down overtime, every member of the Staff must be prepared to work such overtime as may be necessary, particularly in connection with country jobs, but the total working hours to be returned for any day must not exceed 10, and permission to work overtime must be obtained beforehand from a Partner.

The payment (if any) to be made for overtime will be entirely within the discretion of the Partners and will depend upon the general nature of the service rendered by the Assistant. Payment (if any) will be made as soon as possible after the ensuing 31st March . . . (In Nassau Street overtime is paid for at time and a quarter on the basis of the Assistant's salary at the end of the year.)

National Health & Unemployment Insurance:

In Nassau Street the Employers' and Employees' contributions are both paid for by the Firm, so that some adjustment will require to be made on the amalgamated business ceasing to pay the Employees' contribution.

Revision of Salaries:

Salaries to be revised annually not later than 30th April, except in the case of Assistants engaged on trial on provisional terms for the first two or three months. The maximum salary for Typists with over ten years' continuous service to be raised to £180 . . .

Articled Clerks

It is suggested that a certain number of places should be reserved for capable Clerks, and that as regards others

AMALGAMATION WITH MACKIE'S, 1924-29

the premium might be fixed at £ payable (if so arranged) in instalments, while the Articled Clerk might receive in his first year £24; in his second year £36; in his third year £48; in his fourth year, not less than £60, and in his fifth year not less than £72.[7]

TIME RECORDS AND CLIENTS' ACCOUNTS:

(1) Everyone except Mr. Telford and those in the Cashier's Department should prepare a complete daily time record. [There follows detailed description of the various forms A, B, C, and D showing how the weekly forms are cumulated into Client Time Summaries]

(10) Before the Clients' Time Summaries ... are transferred from the current Clients' Time Summary Filing Cabinet, the necessary particulars should be entered in Form E of which a copy should be inset opposite each Client's Account in the Clients' Loose Leaf Ledger. This sheet, which is of a purely statistical nature, enables the Partners at a glance to follow the history of any Account as regards the amount of time spent on each Audit; the proportion of highly priced to lower priced time; the desirability of reviewing the Fee, etc.[8]

(11) The foregoing system has worked with great smoothness in Nassau Street for years and has greatly facilitated the making up of the Firm's Accounts

---

[7] The amount of the premium was left blank. Mackie is here recommending that some of the two articled clerk places per partner be reserved for 'impecunious men of talent'. This was certainly the practice later.
[8] Against this suggestion, a pencilled comment read '? value of this practice'. Paragraph (11) below makes it clear that Mackie expected some opposition from the Craig Gardner side on the point.

at the end of the financial year when no difficulty was experienced in placing a fair valuation on Work in Progress.

(12) It is suggested that Mr. Scott should be provided with an Assistant, (say) Miss Kinnear, to enable him to deal not only with the time records of the amalgamated business, but also to furnish the Clients' Accounts, subject of course to the instruction of the Partners . . .[9]

PROPOSED DEPARTMENTALISATION OF THE BUSINESS:

(1) The Departments might be distinguished as follows:

Mr. Telford	— A.
Mr. Tulloch	— No. 1
Mr Mackie, including the Income Tax Department	— No. 2
Mr. Brock	— No. 3
Mr. Russell	— No. 4
Mr. Shott	— No. 5
Mr. Davy	— No. 6
Mr. Wright	— No. 7
Mr. Scott	— No. 8

---

[9] Mr Scott was Craig Gardner's Cashier who continued as such for many years, finally retiring in the 1960s. Miss Kinnear's name is underlined in pencil, and 'No!' written into the margin.

[... the next few paragraphs contain various transitional procedures relating to the schedules of jobs, but then Mackie suggests a major decentralising of the system.]

(6) On the concentration of the entire business in Dame Street:

> (a) Let the Work Book in Mr. Telford's room be maintained on the principle that *everything shall pass through it*, but alter the heading 'Assistant' to 'Department' and let the Heads of Departments complete the column headed 'Finished'.
>
> (b) Open a Work Book in each of the Departments 1 to 7.
>
> (c) Terminate the present system under which the Senior Assistants wait around the open door of Mr. Telford's room every morning with the object of making 'verbal reports' which, in the circumstances of the case, are largely perfunctory but which waste the time both of Principals and Staff while preventing anything like private consultation on the part of the Partners. Instead of this arrangement let the head of each Department take his Senior Assistants into his confidence as to work in hand and impending, and encourage them not only to plan out the work so that no time will be lost in passing from job to job, but also to enlist the services of Junior Assistants so as to keep down the cost of the work on the job.

In such conditions as are indicated above, Mr. Telford would soon obtain the relief to which he is entitled, as his supervision would be largely confined to watching the 'Finished' column of the main Work Book and keeping his Colleagues up to scratch! ...

The final paragraphs of the eleven page memo cover various miscellaneous items, such as a suggestion that 'to avoid ... the chances of mistakes' typists address their own envelopes rather than leaving it to the Cashier's Department. Stocktaking reminder notices were to be issued to clients, and registers be prepared showing the approximate dates of town and country audits, 'with a view to making some provision beforehand and spreading the Country work over a greater number of Clerks'. Audit clerks were to be 'instructed in every applicable case to prepare a three-year tabular statement, to work out the percentages of Gross Profit, etc., and to obtain explanations as regards all items which appear to be out of proportion'. Clerks were also instructed to study the requirements of the Inland Revenue Authorities in respect of each audit with which they were entrusted, so that they could obtain the detailed information the Inspector was likely to want.

As well as the changes in various office systems, there were more fundamental changes. The Craig Gardner side had no qualified men who were not partners. Mackie's, on the other hand, had two Associates not in Practice, one of whom, Davy, acted as the Office Manager of the new firm. In the latter half of the 1920s, under the influence of John Mackie, Craig Gardner began to recruit qualified accountants. The most plentiful source of these was Scotland, whence George Tulloch and John Russell had already come. Because of an over-supply of Scottish accountants, the starting salary for a qualified man in Glasgow at that time was only £80, whereas they could get £300 with Craig Gardner's.

The first of the new wave was Mr Duthie, who was followed in 1927 by James Walker who subsequently went to the Belfast office and eventually became a partner. William Trotter worked most of his time in Craig Gardner's on the Hospital Sweepstake. W.S. O'Neill worked for some time in the income tax department, before becoming General Manager of Johnston, Mooney & O'Brien. Another import from Scotland was David Stewart, who after some

Amalgamation with Mackie's, 1924-29

years with the firm became Chief Accountant to the Irish Omnibus Company which was subsequently taken over by the Great Southern Railway and then became part of CIE, where Stewart became Traffic Manager. These were early examples of the use of chartered accountants in the offices of major companies, a use which eventually was to change the profession radically. Not only did it allow newly qualified men to choose between professional and corporate life, but it also meant that the quality of accounts presented for audit became much more sophisticated.

Among other changes introduced at this time was the employment of graduates. This was quite a departure: many of the older accountants thought that the young men could learn their business only in the office, and that a university degree was no help. This advice was frequently given to parents who thought of accountancy for their sons. The first graduate clerk was David McCloy Watson, a mathematics scholar from Trinity, who was articled in 1925 and who qualified in 1928. Then came Michael M. Connor, who had an M.Comm from University College, Dublin, and who eventually became Accountant to the Industrial Credit Corporation on its foundation in 1933. William Cunningham, also from Trinity, who had played golf with Beckett while they were at TCD, and Gerard O'Brien, a commerce and economics graduate from UCD, joined the firm in 1927. The long-term impact of these recruits can be assessed by the fact that throughout the 1950s and 1960s Watson, Cunningham and O'Brien were to be the driving force in the firm. They each in turn became senior partner. Another innovation was the employment of women in articles. The first in the firm was Emma Bodkin, sister of Dr Thomas Bodkin, director of the National Gallery (1927-35). She qualified in 1928, the third woman to do so in the Irish Institute.

Despite John Mackie's careful planning and obvious consideration for Telford's wish to become less involved, the amalgamation between the two firms took time to settle down. The differences in style between them were deep-rooted, as a story the somewhat dour Scots Presbyterian John Russell used to tell indicates. Russell visited one of Craig Gardner's country audits for the first time around the middle of the day. He was shown into an office, and followed by a tray of drinks.

'Where are the ledgers and so on?' he asked.

'Why are you bothering about the books?' came the confident reply. 'Craig Gardner's *always* start this way.'

The distinction between the two firms continued for many years, with jobs and clerks being clearly identified as from one side or the other. Gerard O'Brien, who was articled to Mackie, recalls being asked to help with some work for the Secretarial Department, and being discovered doing so; Mackie immediately complained to Tulloch, saying:

'What do you think you're doing using my clerk to write envelopes?'

O'Brien was immediately taken off the envelopes and sent out to the audit of a coal merchant's in Skerries.

At a lower level there was some feeling between the older, unqualified, Craig Gardner men, and the new Mackie recruits. It was not until some years later that the graft between the two firms could be said to have thoroughly 'taken'.

Working Styles in the 1920s

Between 1914 and 1920 Ireland had experienced a period of unprecedented prosperity, as a result of the special market conditions created by the war. The economy was still predominantly agricultural, with up to 80 per cent of production derived from the land, so when agricultural prices rose during the war to nearly three times what they had been in 1912, the economy as a whole boomed. Unfortunately the high prices came down very quickly after 1920, and by 1923 they were half their peak. Ireland,

1915-1940 DUBLIN FEES & PARTNERS % OF FEES

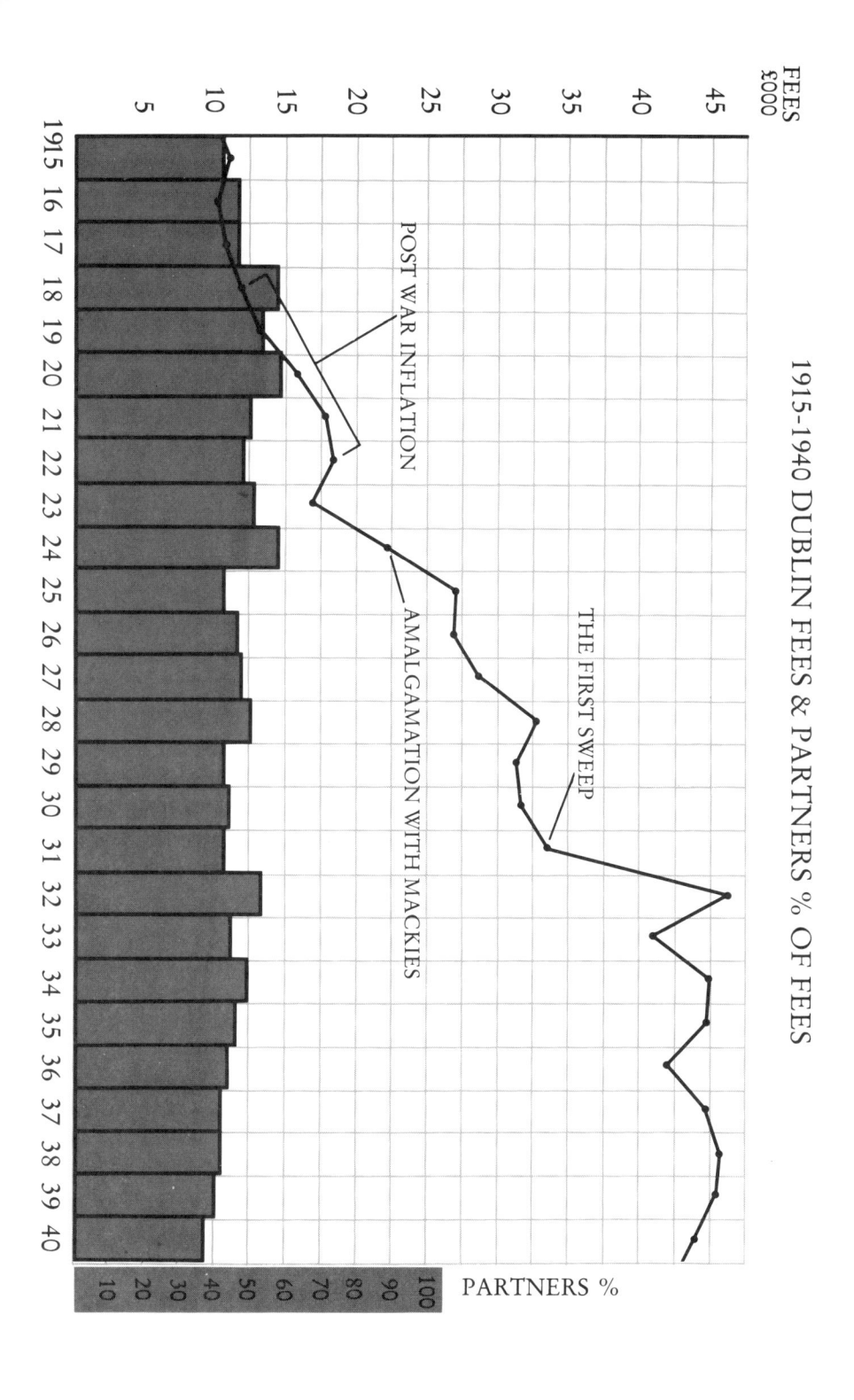

POST WAR INFLATION

AMALGAMATION WITH MACKIES

THE FIRST SWEEP

especially the south, began a depression that was to last, with respites, for the next thirty years.

The output of the agricultural sector did not increase significantly over the decade, and was to be severely hit by the Economic War of the 1930s. This held back other forms of economic development. The prospects for industrial expansion anyway were not good; raw materials and fuel were not readily available, there was no industrial tradition, skilled labour was scarce. There were fewer than two thousand limited companies in the Free State, of which one in six was foreign based. A mere 13.5 per cent of the working population were in industry, only slightly more than the ten per cent working in domestic, hotel and personal service. Sixty per cent of what industrial production there was, was based in Dublin city and county. The slow development of the industrial sector limited the scope for the profession, and the 1926 Census revealed that there were just over seven hundred men and women working as professional accountants. Only a small proportion of these, of course, were chartered. The same Census recorded over seven thousand lawyers, and nine hundred dentists. Craig Gardner, after the Mackie amalgamation, employed 55 accounts staff and 17 secretarial and other staff.

The fee income of the Dublin office rose rapidly, at least in cash terms, after the war, reaching £18,000 by 1922. In real terms however this figure was less than the equivalent in 1914. By 1930 the fee income reached £31,817. The main contributor to this rise was the Mackie partnership, which brought an immediate increase in turnover of £7,500, as well as no doubt a new stream of contacts. Thus, having dropped back during the war, real fee income doubled between 1924 and 1930, and at the end of the decade was 81 per cent more than it had been in 1914. The contribution from the Belfast office moved strongly ahead in the early 1920s, in one year reaching £8,400, a level that wasn't hit again until the 1950s. By 1924 the contribution from Belfast had stabilised at £4,000 where it stayed until the depression of the early 1930s brought it down again.

John Mackie's memorandum about the amalgamation makes it clear that the organisation of the office was based round three functions: audit, income tax and secretarial work. The base of the pyramid was the audit, and the clerk in charge very often did the income tax as well; Gerard O'Brien, for instance, recalls doing P.J. Carroll & Co.'s tax work, including negotiating with the Inspector, as a continuation of the audit function. There was very little departmental specialisation at this time. Liquidations had always been a significant source of income, but they could not be planned for, so the partner, whose liquidation it was, tended to take clerks to help him from whoever was unoccupied at the time. They were in any case not numerous: in 1929 there were only 58 companies in the process of liquidation in the whole Free State.[10] Although some staff, including O'Brien, tended to do liquidations more often than others, there was certainly no specialised department.

New company work was also not plentiful. 'Companies were being registered at the rate of about a hundred a year in the 1920s, but they were almost all small concerns. For the period 1922-30 only 50 public companies were registered, sixteen of which filed a prospectus, and they had an average nominal capital of £78,000 . . . it appears that only one public issue of shares took place during the entire period and that was for the sum of £15,000.'[11]

The small size of the qualified profession, the five-year non-graduate apprenticeship and the restriction of partners to only two apprentices at any time meant that it was not easy to get a placement as an articled clerk. As a result, as Gerard O'Brien recalls, 'there was no such thing as open recruiting — you had to know a partner

---

[10] Bankruptcy Law and Winding-up of Companies Amendment Committee *The Winding-up of Companies and Societies* (Dublin 1929).
[11] W. Thomas *The Stock Exchanges of Ireland* (Liverpool 1986) p 184.

to get a place.' O'Brien's father, as Chairman of the Revenue Commissioners, was of course well known in the profession. William Cunningham was introduced by David Mack, General Manager of the Royal Bank, himself an ex-Craig Gardner man. Once accepted, there was the question of the premium, which at £150 was considerably more than the average annual industrial wage of £118 per year. Apprenticeship fees for the professions varied widely: Todd Andrews, in his *Man of No Property*, describes the average apprenticeship fee for accountants as £200, and for solicitors the fee could vary from £50 in a small firm to as much as £1,000, which did not include the £80 stamp duty paid to the Law Society. Membership of the Stock Exchange cost 1,000 guineas from 1925, plus an annual charge of £50.[12] The premium in Craig Gardner's varied somewhat in the 1920s, but by the 1930s had settled down to £150, and nineteen such fees were paid in that decade. The firm eventually abolished the premium in 1957.

The routine of training and development of articled clerks established in the 1920s was to remain the pattern for nearly forty years. For the first weeks the new clerk was put into the charge of a senior (virtually all the seniors at this time were unqualified), and put to totting great columns of figures or checking postings, with clearly marked ticks in specially coloured ink, so the check could be followed. Much store was put on vouching large and small items of expenditure.

At this time, and for years afterwards, the staff in clients' accounts departments were predominantly book-keepers rather than accountants, and so the audit clerks usually had to draw up trial balances and take the analysis on to profit and loss account and balance sheet. 'The usual audit started from more or less good records — very, very rarely

[12] Average industrial wage for 1926 from *Statistical Abstract* 1931 (Dublin 1931); information about solicitors' fees from Daire Hogan.

did you get accounts made up for you. One often had to write up the books from scratch.' One consequence was, as William Cunningham put it, that professional accountants 'did very little auditing as such, as opposed to preparing the accounts.' The final accounts of most concerns, even very large companies, were typically written up at this time by the auditors. The story is told of a clerk arriving for the annual audit to a country place in the 1930s and asking cheerfully:

'Well, how have you been doing?'

'We're waiting for you to tell us that,' came the reply.

Every morning at 9.30 the junior clerks would report to the office boy who solemnly wrote their time of arrival into the attendance book. The seniors would arrive later, and before 10.00 the audit team would sally out together. This system of daily reporting was not abolished until 1961. For a country job one went down by train on Monday, with an advance (not necessarily used for that purpose) to cover first class travel. An occasional perk of the job was a free lunch, provided by the client. Some places provided snacks at eleven and tea as well. O'Brien recalls working on the audit of the Clarence Hotel with an unqualified senior, who was clearly enjoying the three free meals a day, and intended to spin the audit out. One day O'Brien was sent home at 4 o'clock:

'Off you go,' he was told, 'you've done too much today already.'

After six or twelve months the new clerk would be given small accounts jobs — called 'brown paper parcel jobs' in accountancy firms throughout the world. These were mostly charities, hospitals, and small businesses, some of which kept two sets of books in annual alternation, so that Craig Gardner could work at their leisure on last year's accounts without disturbing the current work.

Many of the brown paper parcel jobs would consist of no more than last years accounts, a cash book, a set of bank statements for the year, and some vouchers in a shoe-box.

These jobs were often used to fill in the non-peak period of the more serious audits, such as the stores, whose year-end of January 31 was a major peak in work-load. The slackest period was October and November, during which time the clerks were supposed to be studying for their exams.

The partners generally kept an eye on their apprentices, but not to the extent of teaching them anything specific. 'The partners would help one with a job, but not with training as such', as O'Brien put it. In that respect clerks were left to their own devices; there was a good course in Rathmines Technical College, and a 'grind' run 'by an old fellow in Donnybrook' — his speciality was actuarial science, a regular exam question, though not anything working accountants ever came across in practice.

Apart from audit and accounts work, the clerks helped with liquidations, did clerical work in the secretarial department and worked on the occasional investigation. One fruitful source of fees in the 1920s was back-duty enquiries. Many traders and individuals had felt it their patriotic duty to withhold income and other taxes during the struggle against the British regime between 1919 and 1922. These people were generally not pleased when the Revenue Commissioners of the new state began to demand payment of the same taxes and eventually to set up an Investigation Branch in the department.[13] In 1927 the Minister for Finance, Ernest Blythe, said in his budget speech that there was still up to £700,000 outstanding in arrears, which represented 16 per cent of total income tax revenue, or slightly more than twice the total receipts for corporation and excess profits tax. By 1930, with great trouble and effort, the sum outstanding was reduced to £80,000, but not before the Revenue Commissioners had acquired a lurid reputation in certain quarters.

[13] In a debate in the Dáil in 1930 independent TD Jasper Wolfe (a solicitor) described the 'harrowing scene' at the deathbed of one of his constituents around which 'floated the Income Tax fiends, following that man into eternity.' S. Reamonn *History of the Revenue Commissioners* (Dublin 1981) p 114

In general new business was not easy to get in the 1920s. Companies rarely changed their auditors. One client the firm did lose, in 1927, was the jam and confectionery firm of Williams and Woods. This had been taken over by the British firm of Crosse and Blackwell, who put in their own auditors Cooper and Cooper, and later the audit went to Stokes Brothers and Pim. In general only this kind of exceptional circumstance prompted a shift of an audit.

Telford, despite his wide outside interests, had never been particularly active as a business-getter, and the other partners, except for Shott and to a lesser extent Brock for liquidations, were not much more effective.

The identification of the firm as Protestant undoubtedly did present problems. One Catholic joining the firm in the 1920s described how: 'people said to me you're a fool to go into Craig Gardner, you'll never get anywhere there — and they said it to my father too.' In 1922 the Knights of St Columbanus had transferred themselves to Dublin, after a series of attacks by the Orange Order and the Specials on the previous headquarters in Belfast. Its members — 'a preponderance of professional men' — quickly set about righting 'the discrepancies encountered at every level of Irish agricultural, economic, industrial and professional life where non-Catholics were solidly entrenched in positions and occupations which depended on already accumulated capital or goodwill.'[14]

The accounting profession did not escape the attention of the Knights. In November 1925 steps were taken by the Knights to inaugurate an Irish Accountants' Society to prevent the flow of money from Ireland by way of fees and to explore the extent to which 'non-Catholics resident within and outside the *Saorstát* were appointing Irish or local agents and representatives for manufacturing and commercial concerns.' Decoded, this means, as their historian put it, that the Knights 'had their fingers on the

---

[14] E. Bolster *The Knights of St. Columbanus* (Dublin 1979) pp 34, 68.

pressure points of the world of business, of finance and administration'.[15]

It is easy to exaggerate the effectiveness of any secretive organisation, and many non-Knights would have been in sympathy with the idea of stimulating greater Catholic and nationalist involvement in business. The Knights, the Old-IRA and, for instance, former pupils of Clongowes, to take three of many such possible groups, would all have had an interest in this. The members of the Irish Accountants' Society are not disclosed, but Vincent Crowley of Kennedy, Crowley, was auditor of the order during the 1920s and 1930s.

Whatever the cause, the flow of government business to both Craig Gardner and Stokes Bros and Pim was disproportionately small compared to the two firms' size and status. The audit of the first state-sponsored body, the Agricultural Credit Corporation in 1927, went to Thomas Geoghegan (educated at Clongowes and Royal University), the Electricity Supply Board (ESB) went to Kennedy, Crowley in the same year, as did Irish Life Assurance in 1939. The Irish Sugar Company went to Kean & Co., founded in 1886 by a graduate of the Catholic University of Ireland. Reynolds, McCarron (another Catholic firm) got Aer Lingus in 1936 and Purtill's (who had bought Michael Crowley's practice) got the Turf Development Board. The first state-sponsored body of any magnitude that Craig Gardner got was the new state transport authority, Córas Iompair Éireann (CIE), in 1944, and this appointment was no doubt largely influenced by the facts that the firm had done the Dublin United Tramway audit (and the West Clare Railway) for many years, and that Frank Lemass, Secretary of the Tramway Company and Assistant General Manager of CIE and brother of Seán, was an ex-Craig Gardner man.

The banks did not suffer any inhibitions about using Craig Gardner, being themselves still largely Protestant controlled. They were a source of liquidation business.

[15] Bolster pp 57-8.

Among the liquidations undertaken during the 1920s were the City of Dublin Steampacket company, whose ships Telford was able to sell off extremely profitably after the war. The company had run the mail boats to Holyhead for many years, as well as cargo vessels, but by the end of the war the fleet had been run down. The cargo ships were sold, and two of the mail boats had been sunk by enemy action. While the company waited to see what compensation the British government would give, there was strong speculation that the directors would decide to wind things up. The liquidation was considered an outstanding success, and Telford's fee amounted to £12,000.

The next important liquidation was that of the *Freeman's Journal*, which finally collapsed after 161 years of publication in 1924. The paper had lost circulation to the *Irish Independent* before the war, and its offices had been destroyed in 1916, and ransacked in 1919 (by police) and 1922 (by de Valera supporters). The liquidation ran until the 1930s; one of the members of the *Freeman's* staff, Johnnie Mackie, was recruited to help with the Hospitals Sweepstake, and became well known as the supervisor at the draws. At the end of the decade Gabriel Brock developed his reputation both in the profession and in the wider commercial world by his contributions as a member of the Bankruptcy Law and Winding Up of Companies Amendment Committee, which presented its final report in 1929.

The partnership of 1924 ran its allotted five years to 1929, but by then it was clear that all was not well between the two senior men, Telford and Mackie. Their characters were widely different: both men had wide outside interests, but Telford's, as we have seen, were, apart from his golf, broadly commercial. Mackie on the other hand was interested in ideological issues. He was involved in the Irish and British Proportional Representation societies, and was Honorary Secretary of the Dublin City and County Liberal Association. The liberal tone of his mind can be seen from his remarks in a paper on proportional representation in Ireland, written in 1927, just before the

Fianna Fáil members re-entered the Dáil, he wrote about the effects of returning to 'first past the post' voting: 'nothing worse could happen which would savour more of injustice to the Republicans. I do not share their views, but to deprive them of the representation to which they are fairly entitled would create a grievance of real substance, and accordingly hinder the peaceful development of the country.' Mackie took a prominent part in the campaign for official registration of accountants, an idea that, though debated in the Oireachtas, came to nothing.

During the 1920s Mackie was President of the Institute in 1925/6 and 1926/7; he was also Vice-President of the Dublin Chamber of Commerce, and in favour of the Shannon scheme. This was a significant point of distinction, on several levels; most businessmen saw the scheme as implausibly grandiose for the new state, which anyway they did not much warm to. There was also a suspicious element of state socialism in the establishment of the ESB as a state-sponsored body, and a high-handed attitude to existing private electricity schemes.

The historian Louis Cullen describes the changes in the Dublin business world during the 1920s. 'It was no longer dominated by the arch-conservative Arnotts, Guinnesses, Martins, or the largely unionist and anglican group who sat on the boards of railway companies and banks . . . the leadership of Dublin business life was shifting away from the old anglican and establishment mode . . .' The new leaders were the Murphys, the Easons and the Jacobs who between them provided Presidents of the Chamber of Commerce in three of the four years 1924-7. The younger partners of Craig Gardner would have had much more in common with the new men than with the old.

Personally, Mackie was, as Gerard O'Brien put it, 'a fussy sort of man — terribly sticky about spelling and such things — he once called me in to his office to say that there was no "e" in lodgment, and he didn't want to see the word spelt wrongly again.'

By the 1920s Telford was in his seventies, and rather

old-fashioned — special arrangements for the amalgamation had to be made to accommodate his letter book, rather than the newer loose-leaf file. A small man, he is remembered by O'Brien as 'a rough, gruff man, who didn't talk much, and was a bit frightening to the young people.' He was also 'a tough little fellow', robust in the Gardner style. His main interest at this time was in the affairs of Portmarnock golf club, where he was one of a ginger group that set up the first Irish Open in 1927, and also restructured the course and the club-house.

It was perhaps inevitable that these two men of a different generation and a different approach to the profession should clash. The specific point of disagreement appears to have been Mackie's objection to Telford's practice of sending accounts to the client for forwarding to the tax inspector rather than sending them direct. Mackie, with his stricter and more professional outlook, took a view of the relationship between the accountant and the inspector, which Telford presumably did not.

In the end Mackie resigned in 1929, and went to London, where he expected to gain some business from the aftermath of one of the great business dramas of the era. This was the failure of financier Clarence Hatry's empire, soon after the exposure of his attempt to buy the US United Steel Company with the proceeds of forged local authority securities. His collapse naturally brought down many connected companies, with associated liquidation problems. Hatry was eventually sent to prison for fourteen years. After working for some time in London, Mackie eventually became ill. He returned to Dublin, where he died in 1940.

CHAPTER 6

THE 1930s AND THE SWEEP

The departure of John Mackie in 1929 left the group of partners in Dublin that remained unchanged until David Telford died in 1943. Two additions were made to the Belfast partnership in this time. Telford remained senior partner of the firm, at least in theory, until his death, with George Hill Tulloch, Edward Buckley (in Belfast), Gabriel Brock, Eustace Shott and John Russell. Until 1935 Telford was paid £2,000 a year, the other shares being expressed as a percentage of the remaining profits: Tulloch 24 per cent, Buckley 25 per cent, Brock 19 per cent, Shott and Russell 16 per cent. A new deed was signed in 1935, bringing James Walker in from the Belfast office, with a 5 per cent share of profits, and reducing Telford's share to £1,000. Tulloch and Buckley had 21½ per cent, Brock 21 and Shott and Russell 18 per cent. Charles Buckley, Edward's son, who had qualified after service in the war, and had worked in South America with Price Waterhouse, was brought into partnership in the Belfast office at the end of the decade. The rest of the staff consisted of five qualified men, ten apprentices, up to thirty unqualified staff and two office boys — some sixty in all.

The stability of the partnership was not to be matched by anything like stability in the economic situation. Craig Gardner's already strong position in the two major areas of accountancy work, company audits and liquidations, meant that the firm had to look to external factors for growth. In the stock market, for instance, Craig Gardner had about twice as many audits as the firm's nearest rival, Stokes Brothers and Pim, and these were the only firms with more than one or two quoted company audits. There was of course no question of attempting to unseat the auditors of non-clients, even if companies themselves had not been reluctant to change. For social and political reasons the firm could not expect much from government-sponsored business, and so, barring extraordinary windfalls, it was to the development of the economy that the firm was obliged to look.

The firm's Dublin fee income had improved steadily but unspectacularly in the late 1920s, moving from

£27,731 in 1925/6 to £31,817 in 1929/30, echoing a 15 per cent rise in the value of national exports, though, as consumer prices fell 5 per cent in the same period, in real terms this was better than it looked. As the great world economic crisis, that was first marked by the collapse of the New York stock market in 1929, hit Ireland, growing unemployment and poverty made the Cosgrave government's political position difficult to sustain. The general election in 1932 put Fianna Fáil in power, an event on which others besides their political rivals looked upon with apprehension. The new government inherited a serious economic crisis. The yield on key 'barometer taxes' such as stamp duty on Stock Exchange transactions, import duty on motor cars, and beer and spirits duties had fallen alarmingly. Consumption of alcoholic drinks had been slipping since 1924, but the retail value of beer and spirits drunk dropped over £2m in 1931/2, more than the fall over the previous five years. Agricultural prices were down and unemployment figures up.[1]

The economic position was not helped by the dispute over payments of the Land Annuities, which resulted in the imposition by the British government of a 20 per cent duty on selected imports from Ireland. In November 1932 Seán Lemass, Minister for Industry and Commerce, prepared a memorandum on the situation for his cabinet colleagues: 'The situation is black ... we have reached the point where collapse of our economic system is in sight. By a collapse, I mean famine conditions for a large number of our people. You will ask how there can be famine in a country which produces more food than it can consume. Famine can come not because our farmers cannot but because they will not continue to produce food.' This somewhat alarmist view was the preliminary to the proposal of a series of radical policies.[2]

---

[1] R. Fanning *The Irish Department of Finance 1922-58* (Dublin 1978) pp 221-2.
[2] Fanning p 247.

Among these policies were the establishment of the Industrial Credit Corporation, restriction of foreign ownership of Irish manufacturing concerns, and wholesale tariff protection. Within a few months the Free State passed from being a predominantly free trading country to one of the most heavily protected economies in the world. At the end of 1931 there were tariffs on 68 articles; by 1936 281 items were covered, and by the end of 1937 it was calculated that 1,947 articles were subject to restriction or control.[3]

The incidence of tariffs was not particularly planned. The onus of proof was put on those who opposed the application, if they happened to find out about it in time. Any firm or group of individuals could make application to have external competition eliminated for their proposed product. As an ex-Secretary of the Department of Industry and Commerce put it 'the work of examination was done principally in the Department and generally in consultation with those interested in the application. Owing to the necessity of preventing forestalling, it was not generally possible to consult the trades interested in the import or sale of the goods in question.'[4] The preparation of the various proposals was a bonus for the accountancy profession, which could not expect much growth from existing clients. One effect was to allow local manufacturers' windfall profits, as they were able to price products at just below the duty-laden imports.

The other side of the protectionist policy was the restriction of foreign ownership of Irish companies. At the beginning of the 1930s there were fewer than 2,000 limited companies registered in the Free State, 92 per cent of

---

[3] J. Meenan *The Irish Economy since 1922* (Liverpool 1970) p 142.
[4] R.C. Ferguson, Secretary of the Department of Industry and Commerce, 1940-45, in *Public Administration in Ireland* quoted in Meenan p 141.

which had capital of less than £20,000. Nearly 60 per cent were in trading or services. New company formation was bumping along at 130 a year. The Industrial Credit Corporation (ICC) began after 1933 to develop financing for local industrial companies, which, combined with the protectionist policies, quickly had a dramatic effect on company formation. In 1934, for instance, 242 new companies were registered, and this rate was kept up throughout the 1930s.

The ICC took a prominent part in the financing and underwriting of new issues on the Dublin Stock Exchange. Between 1934 and 1936 it was involved in 16 out of 42 issues, representing 40 per cent of the capital raised. Craig Gardner was involved with at least five issues in this period: P.J. Carroll, Irish Cinema (which took over the Dublin Theatre Company of which Telford had been chairman), Abbey Clothing, J.H. Woodington, the footware firm, and Independent Newspapers. Stokes Brothers and Pim were involved in three issues, and Kennedy Crowley four.

Most of these issues were heavily oversubscribed, mainly by Irish investors who sold British stocks for the purpose. P.J. Carroll's, for instance, were oversubscribed as much as ten times. Craig Gardner's secretarial department, which handled the clerical side of these matters, was at this time headed by Archibald Wright, and consisted of ten or twelve people. Wright, who was a specialist in company law, was also secretary of various trade associations at the time, including the Irish Timber Importers and the Irish Brewers.

Another aspect of the government's policy was the continuation of the creation of state-sponsored bodies, with thirteen being established between 1932 and 1939. These included Bord Fáilte, Aer Lingus, the Sugar Company, Irish Life and various medical organisations. As we have seen, none of this business came to Craig Gardner.

At the end of the 1920s the firm acquired a job that was to be of major importance for many years. The Hospital Sweepstake audit was acquired through Richard J.

Duggan, the managing director. Duggan was an established bookmaker who had run his first sweep in aid of the 600 victims of the sinking of the *Leinster* by a German U-boat in the last days of the war. In June 1922 he ran a successful sweep in aid of the Mater Hospital, the first of several he and other bookmakers ran, with government permission, in aid of hospitals in the early 1920s. This was a profitable business. Kevin O'Higgins, an inveterate opponent of the sweeps in debate, but who as Minister of Home Affairs was responsible for their conduct, commented drily in the Dáil, 'the carpet of my office is worn out by people whom I never suspected of being philanthropists . . .'[5]

By the late 1920s the voluntary hospitals in Dublin were in a bad way. The value of their endowment funds had been eroded by inflation, and income from new charitable sources was drying up. In 1929 the National Maternity Hospital, Holles Street, threatened to close its doors. A group of hospitals was organised to promote a private member's bill to legalise hospital sweepstakes, and after long lobbying Duggan and others secured the passing of the Charitable Hospitals (Temporary Provisions) Act in 1930.[6] This Act, and the subsequent legislation, set up the National Hospitals Trustees, who in effect employed the Hospital Trust Ltd to run sweepstakes for them. The money was then channelled into the hospitals by the Hospitals Commission. The Hospitals Trust was a private company set up by Duggan, Joe McGrath, who was an ex-IRA politician and labour organiser, and a British engineer called Spencer Freeman. The treasury and audit functions were performed by Craig Gardner, who represented the Hospitals Trustees; the first call on any moneys received was always the Prize Fund and the hospitals fund, with the promoters coming third.

---

[5] A. Webb *The Clean Sweep* (London 1968).
[6] R. Barrington *Health Medicine and Politics* (Dublin 1987) pp 108-9.

The Sweep's success was instant and worldwide. Cartoonist Heath Robinson let his imagination run on the operation of the draw in 1930.

Hospital Trust Ltd set up offices in 13, Earlsfort Terrace, and the staff began to organise the first Sweep, based on the November Handicap. It was a huge success. The prize fund, which had been originally guaranteed at £25,000, and which the promoters privately hoped might come to £125,000, actually reached £417,000. The hospitals got £132,000, and the three promoters received, after expenses, £46,000. The whole of Craig Gardner's staff, qualified or not, worked on the results, often leaving the offices at three or four in the morning, egged on by McGrath. The firm's fee for the first Sweep was £2,205, out of a total for that year of £35,308.

The next Sweep, in March 1931, was on the Grand National, and the receipts (reported net of certain sales expenses, as prescribed in the enabling Act) were £1.7m, and the prize fund £1.2m. Craig Gardner's fee was £2,835 and the promoters' share (reduced from 7 to 2 per cent) was £42,000. A pattern was quickly set whereby the sweepstakes were run three times a year, and (according to the accounts issued after each one to every TD), grossed about £2.75m each time, with total expenses, including the promoters' fees, between 7 and 15 per cent. The rest went in prizes (average £1.75m), and donations to the hospitals, which grossed £17.82m during the 1930s. This was an enormous injection into the health services, considering the total income for voluntary hospitals from other sources for 1933 was £400,000, and the state's expenditure was less than £3m.

The Sweep was an extraordinary phenomenon, from many points of view. In an increasingly depressed, nationalist, and protectionist world economy, people from all over the world took tickets in a sweepstake run in Dublin on an English horse-race for the benefit of Irish hospitals: the global spread achieved from the beginning can be seen by the distribution of the prizewinners of the second sweep, in March 1931. The first prizewinner lived in Battersea, London, the second in Buffalo, New York, and the third in Cape Town, South Africa. Four hundred smaller prizes went to people from Bengal, Alaska,

Surinam, Lisbon, Malta, Manchester, New Jersey, New Zealand, Egypt, Enniscorthy and Cork. By 1934, with joint purchases of tickets, the Sweep promoters noted in one of the Draw programmes that '30 million people were personally interested in the result of every Draw.'

The tickets were not cheap: at ten shillings they represented two or three days work for the average Irish worker — £30 or £40 in 1987 money. Further, in many of the places where they were sold, promotion and participation in lotteries was illegal, and tickets had to be smuggled into the country and sold more or less surreptitiously. It was clear (from the distribution of prizes) that two-thirds of tickets were sold in Britain, where the last state lottery had been held in 1826, and where they were still against the law. This didn't stop Sweep tickets being smuggled into the country in egg-cases, in coffins, in hollowed-out prayerbooks and other ingenious conveyances, but for large-scale distribution the Dublin-Liverpool steamer service was a main route.[7] The sales side was run by McGrath: 'he selected as his staff and departmental heads old IRA-men... Joe knew them, and he proved right.'[8] Because the Sweep was so widely illegal, the sales and distribution operations are clouded in mystery. The internal organisation and the publicity were run by Spencer Freeman. The originator, Duggan, died in 1935.

When the organisation got into its stride, it was selling at least six million tickets for each lottery, three times a year: according to one authority the largest lottery ever held in Britain before that had sold a mere 169,000 tickets.[9]

---

[7] In 1937 a cattle dealer was caught with over £1,000 worth of Sweep tickets in a Gladstone bag. When challenged, 'he released his hold on the bag and dived into the crowd'. He was later charged with importing prohibited goods into the country. *The Irish Times* 24 June 1937.
[8] Jack O'Sheehan, the Hospital Trust press officer, quoted in A. Webb *The Clean Sweep* (London 1968) p 184.
[9] C. L'E Ewen *Lotteries and Sweepstakes* (London 1932) p 351.

The Sweep was above all a marvellous feat of organisation, in which Craig Gardner had various roles. The first was to monitor the number of tickets sold for each sweep and the cash received. The money was in fact lodged by Craig Gardner to a special bank account, and paid over to the promoters as required.

It was a stroke of genius on the part of the Hospitals Trust, though it added considerably to the work, to ensure that everyone who bought a ticket received a personal receipt. This receipt, as well as inhibiting fraud and forgery by agents, had a further effect of stimulating repeat business, so that in the end a hard core of faithful subscribers was built up. The London *Daily Express* marvelled at the efficiency of the organisation in the 1930s: 'a London man who had made a special journey to Dublin called to report that he had not received an official receipt for his 10/- ticket subscription. Within two minutes of his enquiry his card index was produced from among the 3 million-odd names, and he was shown it — his name on a white card, the date he bought the ticket, the date the receipt was posted, and the name of the man from whom he bought the ticket.'

Craig Gardner's next task was to monitor the draw, which was conducted, especially in the 1930s, with the maximum of razzle-dazzle. The counterfoils, up to ten million of them, were taken in a grand procession from the office to the room of the draw, which was originally at the Mansion House, and later at the Plaza Ball Room. Lavish care was devoted to the processions, which typically involved a huge float (one year representing a black cat as big as a house, the next an elephant), and the Garda Siochána band, accompanied by 250 female members of the staff in more or less fantastic costumes.

In 1936 for instance, the Grand National Draw theme was Americana, and the staff were dressed as Hollywood stars, as famous characters in American history, and as the states of the Union. The Mansion House was facaded by a stage set representing the New York skyline, complete with skyscrapers. The Derby draw in June saw two hundred and fifty 'strange and rare fish' parading through Dublin headed by a giant seal, and for the Cambridgeshire Draw of that year the theme was Grand Opera. Several hundred Carmens, Madame Butterflys, Rhinemaidens and other characters escorted the precious counterfoils to the mixing hall. All the costumes and other displays were created by the Harry Clarke Studios.

On arrival the counterfoils had to be thoroughly mixed, so that each of the millions of tickets had an equal chance of selection. Freeman invented a special air blast machine for the purpose. The boxes of counterfoils were solemnly led up to the machine on a special railway, conducted by the jockeys, mermaids, opera characters or whatever. The counterfoils were then put into an eighteen-foot long drum on the stage, by nurses and auditors together, and drawn out by five nurses under the careful eye of the Garda Commissioner. An audience of international journalists (over one hundred were guests of the Sweep in 1931) and spectators watched as each winning counterfoil was drawn from the great drum, and a horse ticket from a smaller drum. Craig Gardner staff were on the stage, recording and supervising every detail of the draw. The whole proceeding took three days or more, as several hundred tickets were picked out in the glare of the most elaborately contrived publicity.

Once the race had been run, and the winners and losers decided, the Craig Gardner Prize Payment Department in Dame Street worked at full pitch to get the prizes out. The receipts had been checked, and several hundred prizewinners had to be notified, and sent a prize claim form. As one member of the staff, who worked in the department in the 1960s, remembered, 'we had ten or twelve people in the department at that time, but even so we had to work overtime for three or four weeks after the race. One problem was that people wouldn't necessarily put their own names on the tickets. Some people put the dog's name, some their children, and we couldn't pay out money to minors.' Every one of the several hundred claim forms had to be counter-signed by a partner, which was one reason why, at least latterly, two partners were always assigned to the Sweep.

The Sweep was an enormous international success almost immediately. It seemed in those depressed days to answer a world-wide need for a chance, however remote, of an escape from the dreariness of everyday life. Not everyone approved, however. Archbishop Gregg of Dublin, the 'principal representative and voice of the church [of Ireland] during the first forty years after independence'[10] disliked the idea intensely. 'The worship of the Golden Calf did not die with Aaron. The "sweeps" are a vast piece of organised solicitation with the direct sanction and support of responsible citizens.' The responsibility of these citizens was terrible. His clergy had told him of the evil effects of sweepstakes on the homes of the people. It would be hard to find anything more cynically callous than this trading upon greed and profiting by the losses of others. 'The most repellent part is that the sweepstakes are for our hospitals.'[11] When a query was put to George Tulloch as to what he felt (as a Presbyterian) about Craig Gardner's involvement in this dubious operation, he remarked dryly: 'It is important that the public be protected by the best professional care.'

The British government, struggling with an economy in trouble, whose citizens were mainly responsible for the success of the Sweep, weren't too pleased either. They set up a Royal Commission and passed an Act prohibiting publicity for 'any lottery promoted . . . in Great Britain or elsewhere' and the activities of selling agents. Fortunately for Craig Gardner the Act did not make the actual purchase of a ticket for one's own use illegal. As a result, after a

---

[10] K. Bowen *Protestants in a Catholic State* (Dublin 1983) p 115.
[11] Quoted in C. L'E Ewen *Lotteries and Sweepstakes* (London 1932) p 366.

momentary hiccup — sales fell from £3.15m in October 1934 to £1.89m in June 1935 — the Act was never a major obstacle, despite periodic police attempts to enforce it.

By this time Craig Gardner's fees from the Sweep had reached £12,000 or more per year, and represented just under 30 per cent of the total fee income for the Dublin office. It was a matter of concern for some of the staff, especially David Watson, who was closely involved in the Sweep, that so much of the firm's income derived from so patently shaky a source. In the event, the Hospitals Trust was to be a steady client for over fifty years. With the advent of postal censorship and other wartime problems in the 1940s, the Sweep's takings, and so the firm's fees, declined dramatically, sinking to 7 per cent of Craig Gardner's fees in 1942. After the war the contribution from the Sweep revived, though it never reached a higher proportion of fees than the 19 per cent of 1955. Until 1963 fees from the Sweep generally represented a more comfortable average of fifteen per cent of total Dublin fees until the mid-1960s, when they declined to less than ten per cent.

Apart from the Sweep the firm was not growing appreciably in Dublin. Non-sweep fees in 1932/3 were £26,992 — almost exactly what they had been in the first year of the amalgamation with Mackie's. This was admittedly a nadir, and was followed by a much better year in 1933/4, but it was not until six years later that they were again to climb to £32,000, a level first achieved in 1927/8. Much of the new business created as a result of Fianna Fáil's policies was going to firms such as Kennedy Crowley, run by Vincent Crowley. Crowley had very good contacts in the business and professional world, one of whom was Arthur Cox, the leading solicitor specialising in business law, who in the early 1960s retired from the firm he had created to become a priest. After assiduous wooing by Eustace Shott, Cox began to send work to Craig Gardner's, and was a good source of insolvency business for years.

The partners in 1939, at a staff outing at Laragh. (From left) *J. Russell, E. Shott, G. H. Tulloch, D. Telford, G. Brock.*

The firm had inherited a prestigious position, and was in all the circumstances, doing well. It was also, as staff remember it, a happy place in which to work. Every summer a day out was arranged; in the late 1930s it was to Laragh, where the partners and their wives would host a tennis tournament, and a dinner afterwards. But, though greatly respected for professional expertise, the firm was perhaps, like other clearly Protestant institutions in the new state, not regarded by the public with much warmth: it was maliciously said that the partners refused to hang bunting out of the windows of the office to mark the Eucharistic Congress in 1932 — and since George Tulloch also objected 'on the grounds of expense' to a papal flag being displayed outside the Arts Club, of which he was a prominent member, perhaps there was something to the story.[12]

Despite the religious identification, one of the great characters of the firm at this time was the cashier, Tom Scott, who was a devout Catholic. Scott is remembered as a large man with a loud voice, which he used vigorously to keep the messenger boys in order. He was also in charge of the stationery cupboard, and in this he established a fearsome reputation for parsimony with the firm's property. As one employee put it, 'He wouldn't give you a second pencil unless you produced the butt of the last one, and it had to be less than ½ inch long — and he wouldn't give you a rubber unless the old one was so small you couldn't hold it.'

Another of the firm's characters was David Cecil Telford, the senior partner's son. He qualified after the war, in 1924, but he left the firm in 1935, and set up a business in Cork. He became converted to Moral Rearmament, a confessional movement widely promoted at the time.[13] He

---

[12] The detail about Tulloch and the Arts Club comes from P. Boylan, author of the history of the Arts Club *All Cultivated People* (London 1988).

later worked as an accountant in Dublin on his own, before becoming a Church of Ireland priest. He died, as William Cunningham put it, 'in an atmosphere of extraordinary sanctity'. The hereditary principle, which was so prominent in British and to a lesser extent Irish professional firms, never became established in Craig Gardner. Very few children of Craig Gardner partners have become prominent in the firm, and since the 1970s it has been a policy that they should not be offered employment by the firm.

In 1935 Tulloch was made a Director of the Bank of Ireland, the first chartered accountant to achieve the position. The firm's staff bonus account's holding of Bank of Ireland stock was used as his £2,000 shareholding qualification. However the post did have a disadvantage. The Belfast Bank, noticing that Craig Gardner now had three partners who were directors of rival banks (Tulloch at the Bank of Ireland, Brock at the Provincial and Telford at the Royal) decided that the time had come to change auditors. Thus, though Tulloch himself was described by the Chairman at his final AGM as 'most agreeable and helpful', the association that had been formed at the beginning of compulsory audits for banks in 1879 came to an end. The bank decided to go outside Ireland for the replacement, and chose the Glasgow and London firm of Thompson, McLintock.[14] The firm's auditing connection with the Provincial Bank had been personal to Sir Robert, and ended on his retirement.

In 1937 Tulloch made a tentative foray into politics. As Robinson put it: 'When the new constitution of Eire came into operation on 29th December 1937, the Institute applied for registration, and was registered, as a nominating

---

[13] It is said that under the stress of this movement he attempted to return his parchment, on the grounds that he had cheated in his exams! The Institute somewhat embarrassedly refused his request.
[14] N. Simpson *The Belfast Bank 1827-1970* (Belfast 1975).

body for the Senate, and George Hill Tulloch and P.J. Purtill were nominated for membership, but neither on this occasion, nor later, was any member nominated by the Institute elected to the Senate.'[15]

On the professional level, Gabriel Brock was important in the affairs of the Institute. He represented Ireland (with Arthur Muir from Belfast) at the International Congress of Accountants in New York in 1929, in London in 1933 and in Berlin in 1938. Perhaps the most important of these was the London Congress, whose proceedings were described at the time as 'a contribution of the first importance in the world of accountancy. They reveal clearly that the profession is moulding definite principles in regard to the important problems involved in the Royal Mail case.' This case, which turned on the use of secret reserves to bolster reported profits, was even twenty years afterwards described as 'the most significant landmark in the life of the profession during the period . . . which fell like an atomic bomb, and changed the face of the world of accounting.'[16] The comfortable world of hidden reserves, which the profession, conscious of the failure rate of companies in the early days of incorporation, could justify on conservative grounds, had been rent apart by misuse of the facility. The shock, and the effects on investors, was equivalent to what would have happened if companies had been obliged to abandon cash based reporting for some form of inflation-related accounts in the 1970s.

In 1938, the Golden Jubilee year of the Institute, Brock became President, after 'Stanley Stokes and John Sedgwick had generously made way so that Gabriel Brock, on whose advice and energy the Institute had so largely depended

---

[15] H. Robinson *A History of Accountants in Ireland* 2nd edn (Dublin 1983) p 124.
[16] F. de Paula 'The Accountant in Industry' in *Sixth International Congress on Accounting* (London 1952) p 235.

for a number of years, should be president on this noteworthy occasion. The celebration included ... a banquet at the Gresham Hotel, Dublin, enjoyed by over two hundred guests, including two (David Telford and William Hayes, Solicitor) who had attended the inaugural dinner in November 1888 and both of whom were prevailed upon to recall that momentous occasion.'[17]

In 1935 Gerard O'Brien was appointed Lecturer in Accountancy in University College, Dublin, having been stimulated to apply by the Professor of Political Economy, George O'Brien (no relation). This was the beginning of a long connection between Craig Gardner and UCD, which subsists to this day, the present Professor of Accounting, Des Hally, having qualified in the firm. Although there was still some doubt about the value of university education for a business career, graduates of the UCD commerce course of ten years before (of whom O'Brien was one) were beginning to make their mark. Todd Andrews was Managing Director of the Turf Development Board (which later became Bord na Móna), Jerry Dempsey, after starting in Kennedy Crowley, became Secretary and later General Manager of Aer Lingus, and James Beddy was Managing Director of the Industrial Credit Corporation. The Commerce Department of UCD was for decades the most significant place where anything like management or business education at university level was available to Catholic undergraduates.

As commercial law and practice became more sophisticated, and as intelligent men and women increasingly went to university as a matter of course, it became essential for the survival of the firm that it recruit an increasing number of graduate entrants. Not only was the tax system becoming more complex and important, but the accounting problems arising from the Hatry case (1929) and the Royal

[17] Robinson p 124.

Mail case drew attention to a series of intellectual issues that had not been addressed by the essentially practical fathers of the profession. Questions arose as to the form in which the accounts of holding companies should be presented, how the profits and losses of subsidiaries should be dealt with, depreciation, valuation of stock in trade and the amount of disclosure in published accounts. One of the leading intellectuals to discuss these issues was Frederick de Paula, ex-Professor of Accountancy and Business Methods at the London School of Economics and at this time Controller of Finance at Dunlop.

In 1933 he, with joint auditors Stokes Brothers and Pim, and the British firm Whinney, Smith and Whinney, produced the landmark Dunlop accounts, which included for the first time in a British company both a consolidated balance sheet and a consolidated profit and loss account. But apart from the Dunlop accounts, there was little chance to practice these new techniques in Ireland, since they depended on the establishment of holding companies such as had resulted from the merger movement in America in the 1900s and in Britain in the 1920s. Not until the 1950s and 1960s was this to be a feature of the Irish business scene. The slow development of industry in the country, and the fact that auditing and the preparation of final accounts were invariably done together, meant that audit technique developed slowly in Ireland. Additions to technique often came after some mischance had revealed a problem: the examination of paid cheques, for instance, developed after work on a back-duty case in the country revealed a large fraud that had been sustained over the previous ten years. Other factors hindered the development of technique: thus it was not Craig Gardner's practice until the late 1930s to circularise debtors, for fear of casting doubt on the client's solvency (even then the form required the debtor to respond only if things were wrong, leaving a theoretical confusion between approval and non-response). The secretiveness of the times was also a factor: as late as 1963, when *Notes on Audit and Accounting Requirements of the Companies Act 1963* was prepared, it was carefully labelled 'For guidance of and use by members of the staff', and the copies numbered so that the distribution could be controlled.[18]

Except for the Sweep, the 1930s were not a particularly successful era for the firm. Fee income was not buoyant, and after 1935 salaries crept up: they were 48 per cent of Dublin fees in 1930-35, but rose steadily in the second half of the decade to 56 per cent in 1936/7 and 1937/8 and 58 per cent in 1938/9 and 1939/40, higher than they had ever been. This movement was of course reflected in the partners' profits. In 1931/2 they exceeded 50 per cent of income (including the Belfast contribution) for the last time in the period covered by this history; a few years later (1938/9) they had sunk to 40 per cent of income for only the second time in the century. The previous occasion was in 1914, but on that occasion they had quickly recovered — the ratio in 1938/9 was the precursor of lower levels still. The senior partner, Telford, was now in his eighties, and Tulloch, his successor, was in his sixties. The firm had no certain entrée into the new sources of business of the time. Like most professional men of their time, the partners were not people who went out vigorously looking for business; the firm tended to live on its position. As a result, when the Second World War broke out, hitting the Sweep in particular and the Irish economy generally, the firm felt it.

---

[18] By contrast, the latest edition, on the 1986 Companies Act, is on public sale.

CHAPTER 7

THE LONG EMERGENCY OF THE 1940s

B y 1940 the Dublin partnership consisted of the older men, David Telford and George Hill Tulloch; Gabriel Brock, whose banking interests were taking an increasing amount of his time; John Russell, a shrewd but not vigorous man; and Eustace Shott. Shott had been for some time the key to the firm's survival. He had become a partner in 1924, and was an outgoing, gregarious man, a golfer and a champion bowler. He was greatly respected in the business community, particularly by clients who felt that he understood their problems, and that they could look to him for help. This help included tax-planning, of which he was an early exponent.

The first impact of the worsening international situation was felt in May 1939, when the accounts for the Derby Sweep reported takings down 30 per cent on the previous year. The next Sweep, in October, was 45 per cent down on the previous year, and by August 1940 takings had dwindled to £91,000, a mere 3 per cent of their peak in the 1930s.[1] Naturally this was reflected in Craig Gardner's fee earnings from the Hospitals Trust, which collapsed from a peak of £12,950 in 1938 to £2,900 in 1941, by which time they represented only 7 per cent of fees. The great offices of the Hospitals Trust in Ballsbridge were let out to the Department of Supplies for the duration of the Emergency.

The decade started memorably for the firm, with Shott being concerned with a major liquidation, that of Clery's. This great shop had already been liquidated by Craig Gardners some sixty years before, when Robert Gardner sold what had been McSwiney's and then the Dublin Drapery Warehouse to M.J. Clery of Limerick for £32,000. Clery came from Cannock's of Limerick, which was, like

---

[1] Spencer Freeman spent the war in Britain, working for Beaverbrook's Ministry of Aircraft Production. He returned to Ireland in 1945 with a CBE.

the Drapery Warehouse, a client of the firm's. Gardner's fee for the liquidation was £1,000. By 1939 the company's profits had been declining steadily for five years, and showed losses in the year ending January 1939 and January 1940.[2]

The company was in trouble. The Chairman, Sir Christopher Nixon (who had married Miss Louise Clery, in 1917) advanced £20,000 to the company, and attempted to sell the premises, but failed. As creditors pressed, and the board talked of liquidation, the staff offered to accept lower wages and a reduction in numbers. The board then asked the Equity and Law Life Assurance Society, which had lent the company £200,000 secured by a debenture, to put in Eustace Shott as Receiver.

Because of the long connection between the two firms, the board, somewhat naïvely, saw Shott and Craig Gardner as allies in their cause. They intended to use the receivership as a way of staving off the company's creditors while they looked for further finance. Unfortunately for the board, Shott quite correctly took the view that as Receiver he was particularly responsible to the debenture holder, and he thought it his duty to dispose of the assets and discharge the debenture for the benefit of the Society. Some of the animus against Shott that can be read between the lines in the subsequent litigation can be traced to this misreading by the board of how appointment as Receiver necessarily changed Shott's focus of attention.

As soon as he was appointed, Shott sought a purchaser for the shop. This was easier said than done. The company had liabilities, apart from the debenture, of £143,000, and was trading at a loss. It was, moreover, largely dependent for its turnover on imported goods, which were not going to be a high priority of the Department of Supplies

[2] *Irish Industry — The Business Journal of Ireland* November 1941.

while the war lasted. Shott set up a committee of the trade creditors to advise him, a very unusual step for the time.

Negotiations with prospective purchasers were put in hand, but were proving slow. It became clear that much of the stock was old, and had been valued too highly on the balance sheets. In November Shott asked the advice of Denis Guiney, who was clearly making a great success of his drapery shop in Talbot Street. Though at first unenthusiastic, Guiney made an offer two days later to purchase Clery's as a going concern for £225,000. He had not valued either stock or premises in detail. The offer was on a take-it-or-leave-it basis, and Guiney demanded a quick decision, taking the view that the longer the business was left inactive the more difficult it would be to revive, and that to miss the crucial Christmas season would significantly lengthen his payback period. Guiney insisted on a decision on his offer by 15 November. Shott called a creditors' meeting, which eventually accepted a slightly raised offer giving them 1/- in the £. In the event this money was handed over by the creditors to the staff, many of whom had deposited their savings with Clerys and were therefore badly hit.

Sir Christopher Nixon, who was still trying to find money, was told of the offer and the Receiver's intention to accept it. By 29 November the shop was open again for business, with a great sale that realised £54,000 in the first week. At the end of the month the old board started proceedings against Shott and Guiney to set aside the sale, on the grounds that the price realised was insufficient, that the assets should have been sold separately in order to realise a higher price, that the Receiver had stampeded the sale through, thus preventing the board from coming to a better arrangement with their bankers, and that the price was fixed with a view to covering the debenture and the expenses rather than with the actual realisable value of the assets in mind.

In the event Mr Justice Gavan Duffy in the High

Court decided the case wholly in the Receiver's favour.[3] The judge failed to see any merit in the idea of a value in the property beyond that of the market value, defined as the market value at the time of sale. In court Sir Christopher had expressed the view that Clery's was 'a goldmine sold at a scrap price'. The judge didn't take this valuation too seriously, since Sir Christopher had himself failed to make a profit on the enterprise. As was pointed out, no one came forward to pay more than Guiney, 'yet such a witness would have been of far more practical value than the most glowing description of the finest site in the capital.'

Shott had clearly taken some risks in accepting Guiney's offer in such haste. The judge said that Mr Guiney's methods in the purchase 'were as unorthodox as they were direct. He consulted no valuer, brought in no accountant, required no special stock-taking . . . he did not trouble to examine the Company's accounts.' But this did not mean that Shott had been negligent or wrong in accepting the offer. The judge was more critical of Shott's accepting a 'casual' opinion as to the valuation of the premises from a specialist whom he had consulted 'very informally indeed'.

What Craig Gardner's thought of the Clery's case was summed up by the office poet (Shott's secretary Mary Doran), in a verse delivered to the office party.

Denis Guiney Saying His Prayers

Dear God, Oh teach me how to pray,
That I may praise thee night and day,
For all thy blessings shown to me
O Lord I thank friend Shott and Thee.

---

[3] Gavan Duffy J.'s unreported judgment in *Clery & Company* v *Shott and Another* 8 May 1941, copy in Craig Gardner.

The crowds outside Clerys for Denis Guiney's first great sale, in November 1940.

A History of Craig Gardner & Co.

Dear God, for all Thy blessings shed
Upon my undeserving head
I'll daily thank Thee more and more,
But most for Christy Nixon's store.

Dear God, I got an awful fright,
When Christy Nixon said he'd fight.
But Thou O Lord, who sleepeth not
Were watching over me and Shott.

Dear God, You know I judgeth not
But much I fear that Eustace Shott
Is void of grace, outside thy Church
Oh Lord don't leave him in the lurch.

Don't ask me Lord I'd rather not
Tell Thee what Christy said of Shott.
If half be true, then truth to tell,
Poor Shott is heading straight for Hell.

And so O Lord, for my dear friend,
I to Thy Gracious presence send
My prayers, O Lord let them prevail.
Forget not, Lord, the Clery Sale.

Dear God, before I go to bed,
There's one thing more that must be said.
One further blessing I implore,
I want a licence for the store.

Remember Lord thy clergy dear
Who come to Clery's year by year
Recall, O Lord, the days afar
When Clery's had a private bar.

I know O Lord the holy nuns
Are well content with milk and buns,
But sure, O Lord, each parish priest
Would want a ball of malt at least.

The Long Emergency of the 1940s

And so O Lord one blessing more
I on my bended knees implore
The clergy all would like I'd have it
And so O Lord tell Cahir Davitt.[4]

The emergency situation created by the war cut the takings from the Sweep, made Clery's harder to sell, and reduced the office heating system to the smouldering of wet turf. For a firm with so country-wide a spread of business, fuel shortages were a constant headache. The petrol ration for private motor cars was virtually non-existent, and trains were run on turf, wood and 'duff' — a mixture of coal dust and pitch. These were not efficient fuels: the build-up of clinker meant that the fires had to be put out and cleaned as often as every few miles. As a result the train from Dublin to Athlone was regularly overtaken by the barges on the Royal Canal, and on one occasion in 1942 a train took twenty-three hours to travel from Dublin to Killarney. Not everywhere suffered in the same way: staff on the P.J. Carroll's audit in Dundalk were able to use the Great Northern Line which, because it was used in the north for troop transport, was kept well supplied with fuel.[5]

On the other hand the situation did create some new business. The Department of Supplies had been set up in December 1939 to regulate the flow of restricted goods like tea and sugar. Distributors and manufacturers wishing to use rationed goods had to produce an auditor's certificate of their actual usage, and they were then allocated a reduced percentage of that usage, depending on what was available. This activity, which often required monthly

---

[4] Davitt was the District Justice who heard the application for the licence, which was eventually obtained by the shop after a special Act was passed by the Oireachtas.
[5] B. Share *The Emergency* (Dublin 1978) p 53.

factory visits, kept the firm very busy during the Emergency period. Craig Gardner had for instance to certify the usage of sugar by Scott's jam factory, which they did by comparing the actual output with the recipe. Thus raspberry jam required 60 per cent sugar, strawberry 50 per cent and so on.

The firm, and other accountants, were in effect making it possible for the Department to control the supply of goods as fairly as possible. This was the first time that the Irish accountancy profession had been extensively used as an essential instrument of state policy. This kind of involvement, which English accountants had also previously experienced in the First World War, and which had significantly improved the status of the profession there, was carried on in the 1950s by the appointment of Gerard O'Brien to the first Prices Advisory Body.

The increase in tax during the war kept the still quite small tax department busy. In 1941 it became clear to the government that a number of businesses were making substantially increased profits during the emergency, very often because shortages gave an inflated value to existing stocks. As a result excess corporation profits tax was introduced in the budget, whereby any profits over a 'standard' figure would be liable for tax at 50 per cent. Various reliefs and set-offs, relating to companies which had made issues of capital, or moving losses from one year to another, made the tax complicated. However the fact that the similar British excess profits tax was at 80 per cent raised a tax-planning possibility for companies that were basically Irish but which for historical reasons were registered in Britain.

In 1943 David Telford, who had been senior partner for twenty-six years, died, having appointed Brock and Shott as his executors. George Hill Tulloch, who was by now seventy, became senior partner. It had long been clear, at least to Eustace Shott, that new young partners were needed, but the older men had resisted this on the grounds of the uncertainties of the time. Shott also saw the need to break the exclusively Protestant character of the partnership, for as he said to O'Brien:

'You know, O'Brien, it's more than overdue that we had a Catholic partner in this firm.'

In March 1944 both of these objectives were achieved. David McCloy Watson, William Cunningham and Gerard O'Brien, who had joined the firm in the 1920s, were admitted to the partnership. The new partners represented significant changes in the firm: they were the first graduate partners, and Gerard O'Brien was the first Catholic. They were also the first partners to have started their professional life in independent Ireland.

In 1944 six articled clerks qualified in the same year. The course of their careers show the developing range of possibilities open to qualified men. Two of them, Michael Manley and James Russell (himself son of a partner) eventually became partners, another, John Keogh, stayed on as a senior, and three eventually went into industry (Cramptons, Irish Sugar and Hugh Moore and Alexander). Two more clerks qualified in 1945: R.D. Power-Fardy stayed (in the Sweep department) and C.P. Martin, became accountant of Aer Rianta.

The opportunities for qualified men were just beginning to develop outside professional practice, a development which was to change the type of recruit that the profession was able to attract. Of the 102 Associates Not in Practice listed in the Institute's 1945 yearbook as working in Dublin, 49 were in accountancy practice and 48 were in industry (5 unclassified). The relatively new semi-state sector employed several of these. Of those working in accountancy, Craig Gardner employed thirteen qualified people, Purtill's had seven and Stokes five.

Towards the end of the 1940s the Profit Sharing and Saving Scheme in the firm which had been started after the First World War was wound up. Interest on the money accumulated continued to be paid, but the allocation of profit share ceased in 1949. By this time there were only a few of the older unqualified men still in the scheme, one of whom — T.J. Scott the cashier — didn't finally take his money out until 1956, by which time it had grown to £2,350. Except for these few men, the scheme had not been a wide success. After ten years of operation there were eleven men in it, with an accumulation of £5,215. As these men left, the number in the fund dwindled, until by 1940, there were only seven, though the fund had accumulated to £8,500.

Soon after these changes, the firm got its first major state-sponsored body audit — Córas Iompair Éireann (CIE). This was the amalgamation of the Dublin United Tramways (DUTC), which had been a client since before its incorporation in the 1890s, and the Great Southern Railways, which had combined twenty-six Free State railways in 1924. After 1927 the Great Southern had increasingly developed road services as well as rail. The audit of the Great Southern Railway had been done by Price Waterhouse, but ironically in view of the later close connection between the two firms, the partner concerned was less than co-operative with information. As a result the new Craig Gardner partner Gerard O'Brien and a senior had to spend two or three months learning the job. They were helped in this by the CIE staff, especially the accountant, Hartnell Smith (an ex-Price Waterhouse man) who drew up a complete flow chart and plan of all the relevant activities. The assistant general manager, Frank Lemass (brother of Seán Lemass) was well known to the firm both because he had been with the DUTC and because he was himself an ex-Craig Gardner man.

Whatever assistance was available, this was a very demanding audit. Apart from the Sweep, it was by far the largest job the firm had, with a fee of some £1,000, which was four times the normal large company fee. The new company was extremely extensive, with offices all over Dublin, thousands of employees all over the country, and a wide range of activities. Not least of the complications was the difficulty of consolidating the Great Southern Railway accounts, which were based on the old-fashioned double accounts system, as laid down in the Railway Companies

(Accounts and Returns) Act, 1911, and the Tramway company's, which were based on normal commercial forms. The double accounts system had been invented originally by William Deloitte, and first enshrined in legislation in 1868. It involved preparing separate statements of money received, and money expended, on capital account, rather than a summarised version. It also envisaged that no depreciation would be charged, assuming that once the permanent way was established, regular maintenance would keep it in peak condition.[6] Eventually the two forms of account were drawn together in a format recommended to the Minister by Craig Gardner's.

The CIE audit structure soon settled down. A detailed programme was available for each department, probably the first Craig Gardner job for which this was done, and the two seniors and twelve clerks involved were able to base the audit of each department on an overall audit map. Most of the physical auditing relied on certificates, and the meticulous internal audit staff. These station auditors were responsible for checking the activity at the individual stations; their reports however were not confined to financial matters. In the old tradition of the railways they reported on whether the fires were lit in the waiting room, and how the station was kept in general, even down to whether the pennies were removed every day from the penny-in-the-slot locks on the lavatories.

Random personal checks by Craig Gardner staff, such as to one of the hotels, to the Rents office, or to one of the garage depots, were also made from time to time. Much of the audit work however depended on routine checking of postings and bank statements and so on. For the firm the audit had an importance beyond its profitability, which was not great. It was work that could be done outside the peak season, thus easing off-peak staff

---

[6] C.H. Newton *Railway Accounts* (London 1930) pp 8, 178.

management problems; techniques developed and learned on such a large audit filtered down to the smaller ones, particularly as the partners made a deliberate effort to spread the work amongst the clerks; and finally, as the major state-sponsored body audit, it was a symbol of the firm's position in the country.

Towards the end of the war, the Sweep, which for the duration had been held four times a year on behalf of the Irish Red Cross, began to pick up. One cause was the number of American servicemen stationed in Northern Ireland. By 1946 Spencer Freeman was back from his war-work in England, and the structure of large international sweeps held three times a year was re-established. Craig Gardner's Sweep fees in that year went up to £7,750. In 1947 the British *Sunday Pictorial* complained bitterly about this flow of illegal funds to Ireland: 'every visitor to Eire from England, Scotland and Wales — and thousands are arriving weekly — is a potential ticket buyer. Many are returning home with books of tickets to sell . . . additionally to bolster subscriptions from Britain, agents are employed in every part of the country. Their names are on a secret list, and the way they get their books of tickets is never divulged.'[7]

With the end of the war and the revival of the European economy under the Marshall Plan, the firm began to pick up business. In 1945 the fees were £45,000. By 1950 they had risen to £78,000, and they were to continue to rise throughout the 1950s and 1960s. This revival of the economy, which was anyway slow, came too late to help Locke's Distillery in Kilbeggan. This was a very old operation, which claimed to have existed since 1757. The prohibition of whiskey exports during the war had put the firm into trouble, and the distillery was offered as a going concern. The world shortage of whiskey at the time made the firm's

---

[7] *Sunday Pictorial* 27 June 1947.

stocks attractive, and various speculators, including some 'undesirable Swiss nationals', hoped to buy the distillery. In the event the firm wasn't sold, though gossip, apparently quite unfairly, attempted to create a scandal by connecting political figures to some of the potential purchasers.[8]

The general ethos of the firm at this time was still quite old-fashioned. The senior partner, George Hill Tulloch, had after all joined the firm in 1904, and by 1950 was nearly eighty. In the old style, time management was not much regarded. All the clerks, except those on country jobs, reported in to the office every day before going out to work. On country jobs it was required to write to the senior partner every day to inform him of progress. Every Saturday all the articled clerks, seniors and juniors, would queue outside Mr Tulloch's office and report their progress on whatever they were doing. He would if necessary allocate their next week's work. During the week, if a clerk wished to see a partner, he would simply present himself at the office and wait until the partner was able to see him. Not until the late 1950s was it felt necessary, with the mounting pressure of work, to make appointments.

Another mark of the times was the deep penetration of the ethos of confidentiality, a mark that is still important. As a note of professionalism this has a long history: it is mentioned in the Hippocratic oath, that earliest statement of professional ethics. In *Bleak House*, Dickens described the grand family solicitor, Mr Tulkinghorn, as 'surrounded by a mysterious halo of family confidences; of which he is the silent depository . . . noble secrets walk abroad among men, shut up in the breast of Mr Tulkinghorn.' This image, and the reality, is an essential part of the stock-in-trade of the professional man, and, at the same time, this role as knower and keeper of secrets must have been part of the attraction of the professional life. It was also the

---

[8] E.B. McGuire *Irish Whiskey* (Dublin 1973) p 366.

symbol of the much-prized identification of the firm as a firm of integrity.

In the country, of course, the relative confidentiality of the Dublin auditors had long been a reason for having a city auditor. Gerard O'Brien recalls one client, a country landowner, asking that the firm's letters be despatched in plain rather than printed envelopes, to reduce the temptation for the carriers. On a normal audit, clerks were not even supposed to reveal where they were working to outsiders — they could if necessary leave a telephone number, but not the name of the client. Perhaps this particular caution was the last hang-over of the days when having the accountants in was the prelude to bankruptcy, but it fitted in well with the ethos of the time. When the firm recruited for staff, as it did regularly, it was always under a box number. Not until December 1962 did the partners' committee minutes record a 'feeling amongst committee that a certain number at least of Advertisements should be under our own name, especially where we want first class men.' Employees' salaries were a deeply private matter, discussed by the partners only on the basis of hand-written memoranda. After the annual rises had been agreed by the partners, the staff would call on Tulloch, not knowing whether they had been given one or not.

On the other hand the partners' rooms, where job correspondence files were kept, were open to clerks. The relations between the clients and the partners and between the partners and the staff were both more formal than is usual in the 1980s, and more personal. The partners were very conscious in a small city of the need to establish and maintain friendly relations with clients. A new trend at this time was an increasing reluctance for partners to take directorships of companies, a practice that had been quite common in Telford's day. Directorships henceforth tended to be limited to semi-private concerns, particularly family companies, where it was desirable to have a non-family member on the board.

Between the partners there were signs of different approaches to the management of the office. The three younger partners, having had some considerable years as employees of the firm, had their own views on, for instance, employee salary levels, that were not always shared by the old partners. This proved frustrating for the younger partners, especially since they could not persuade Brock or Shott to take a very active interest in these matters. In 1949 Gabriel Brock, who had in 1945 been the first accountant to become Chairman of the Dublin Chamber of Commerce, retired from the firm to become full-time Chairman of the Provincial Bank. A new partnership deed was drawn up, which lasted until 1954. The senior partner was George Hill Tulloch, and the other partners were John Russell, Eustace Shott, James Walker (Belfast), David Watson, William Cunningham, Gerard O'Brien and John McCartney (Belfast). In 1950 the other partners clubbed together and 'as a mark of their appreciation and in celebration of the completion of fifty years since his admission as a member of the Institute of Accountants and Actuaries in Glasgow' presented George Tulloch with his portrait by 'the well-known Irish artist, Mr Leo Whelan RHA, FRSA'[9] as the fitting climax to a long career. He eventually retired in 1954, and died in 1957. Although Tulloch was particularly inclined to be loyal to the established systems, Dr Howard Robinson, who served as an assistant with Craig Gardner from 1937 to 1944, describes him as 'a man of great presence and charm, punctilious to a fault' and notes that 'his care and thoroughness acted as a perfect foil to David Telford's directness and drive.'[10]

In 1954 J.A. Milliken, J.R. Morton, Gordon Buttanshaw and James Russell (John Russell's son) were added.

---

[9] *The Accountant* 14 January 1950.
[10] H. Robinson *A History of Accountants in Ireland* 2nd edn (Dublin 1983) p 384.

At the same time Jimmy Nelson was admitted to the Belfast office.

In 1956 Eustace Shott suffered a heart attack, and was laid up for several months in a nursing home. Eventually, in January 1957, his doctors let him back to work, taking the view that he was better at the scene of action than fretting in bed. A ground-floor room was made available to him, and he began picking up the reins of work. On 15 July he left the office to visit his client Mulcahy Redmond & Co. of Ardfinnan, but he suffered another, and this time fatal, heart attack in Kingsbridge (Heuston) station.

The shock in the firm was tremendous. Shott had for many years been the leading force in the firm, both as a business getter and inside the office. Junior staff regarded him with some awe, not least because his habits of speaking with his pipe constantly in his mouth, and (in the days of two-piece telephones) of conducting a telephone conversation strolling round his office with the earpiece, leaving the voice-piece on his desk, made him sometimes difficult to understand. On the other hand it was he who organised the office parties when they were revived after the war. These were elaborate affairs, with printed menus and 'musical artistes' — for some years they were held at the fashionable restaurant in Dublin airport, and later in various hotels in the city.

For his junior partners, Shott had been crucial to the survival of the firm. He was not a technical accountant, his strength was more as a businessman, but he was very well respected, and not only in commercial circles. Alexis FitzGerald, the solicitor and advisor to the then Taoiseach Mr Costello, credited him with the idea for the Industrial Development Authority. In a letter to *The Irish Times*, FitzGerald wrote: 'the idea of the Industrial Development Authority was given to the Inter-Party Government by the late Mr Eustace Shott then senior partner in the firm of Craig Gardner . . . he handed me a memorandum fully developing the idea in, I believe, the early summer of 1948.

I handed it to Mr Costello who promoted the idea with the Minister for Industry and Commerce of the time, Mr Daniel Morrissey'.[11]

The loss of the strong personalities of Brock, Tulloch and Shott between 1949 and 1957, left only one of the 1924 partnership in the firm, the senior partner, John Russell. In 1958 the Department of Finance published its plan *Economic Development*, and the Irish economy was about to move at a very different pace. With this movement came a significant widening of the services demanded of the accountancy profession. The three graduates admitted to the partnership together in 1944, Watson, Cunningham and O'Brien, were between them to drive the firm into the new era.

---

[11] Shott was not, of course, senior partner — except perhaps in the general perception.

CHAPTER 8

THE BEGINNINGS OF MANAGEMENT

The 1950s were not a comfortable time for the Irish economy. Despite the rising tide of prosperity in Europe and the USA, living standards in Ireland increased by only 12 per cent during the period 1949-56, compared with an OECD average of 35 per cent. Throughout the 1950s, moreover, Ireland experienced emigration on a scale that seemed almost to amount to the failure of the nation. As T.K. Whitaker put it in *Economic Development*, 'after thirty-five years of native government people are asking whether we can achieve an acceptable degree of economic progress.' Fifty thousand people left the countryside every year. Many however went to the cities, notably Dublin, whose population increased by 20 per cent in fifteen years. Most of those who found work found it in administration, in commerce, in financial and personal services and in the professions. Very little industrial development took place before the government's economic policies changed in 1958.

The most vigorous entity in Ireland was the Catholic Church, led in Dublin by the redoubtable Archbishop John Charles McQuaid who set in motion a major church building programme to accommodate the needs of the rapidly growing numbers of the faithful in the city. Politically and socially the Church was at the peak of its influence. In 1951 the government accepted the views of the bishops on the Mother-and-Child Scheme, and throughout the decade the faithful generally were made vigorously aware of the hierarchy's views on various other matters. The number of books banned by the Censorship Board soared to an average of 600 a year between 1950 and 1955. Dance-halls were forbidden to stay open after midnight, it was declared to be a mortal sin to marry a Protestant or attend Trinity without the Archbishop's permission, and plans for an agricultural university (or indeed almost any other state initiative) were denounced as creeping Socialism.

In other ways, also, the Church resisted identification with the state. Immediately after the budget in May 1953 several letters were published in *The Irish Times* discussing whether the Church's moral code permitted a taxpayer to falsify income tax returns. Various zealous Catholic laymen explained, to the evident bafflement of a 'Puzzled Presbyterian' and other Protestant contributors, that 'a Catholic is not required under the moral law to make a complete income tax return.' This was described as 'a commonplace of Catholic teaching'.

The reason lay in the fact that the government, knowing that there will be evasion, fixed tax rates at higher levels than they would need to be if everyone paid up in full. 'The man who pays is entitled in strict justice to himself to take cognisance of this . . . he is morally entitled to hold back part of his income in fairness to himself.' It was no lie to sign an incomplete declaration, since the taxgatherers expected everyone to suppress income and are therefore 'not in any formal sense deceived by an incomplete return, and the essence of a lie is deceit.' Unfortunately the question as to whether a tax advisor may be morally, as opposed to professionally, justified in helping a client to prepare an incomplete return was not discussed.

'T.J.F.' who closed the correspondence with this magisterial analysis, pointed out for good measure that despite the special position of the Church as enshrined in the Constitution, 'the Church cannot do violence to her own principles, even at the risk of appearing ungrateful to benevolent governments.' In this atmosphere it is not surprising that the influence of religious affiliation in economic life was still strong. Most firms were readily identifiable as Protestant or Catholic, and because work was sought and disposed on the basis of family and neighbourhood connections, especially in the professions, people tended to find work among their co-religionists. Positive discrimination was practised on both sides: one insurance company, for instance, 'identified Catholic aspirants by their schooling, and these were put aside.' Only rarely did they need to choose from this secondary list.[1] By 1968, when Craig Gardner appointed the firm's first Catholic senior partner, the atmosphere had changed, and most firms no longer worried about such matters. An employee's religion had become a private matter.

One of the causes of the change was the development of the economy after 1958, and the decline of the exclusively family firm. For Craig Gardner the tight-knit nature of the business world had long been a fact of life: new business was not got by aggressive bidding, which would anyway have been regarded as quite unethical, but by personal reputation and relationships. In 1950 there were 5,734 non-financial limited companies registered in Ireland, of which 6 per cent were public. Sixty-seven Irish companies had a paid-up capital of more than £100,000; in a quarter of these companies family holdings of directors represented over 80 per cent of the shares. In 55 per cent of larger companies family directors held over half the shares. Two-thirds of these Irish companies had one or two family board members. Furthermore the number of families involved was small: 'the Irish business elite of the 1950s was comprised of 107 families', who held significant interlocking holdings in various companies and financial institutions.[2] It is not surprising in this context that the religious predilections of firms should be so clearly defined. On the other hand, under the influence of state and international capital, things were about to change rapidly. The intimate, personal style of control was quickly to change to a more impersonal, managerial style. This change naturally required that professional firms serving the new business world should also change their style.

In 1957 regular and more or less formal partners' meetings were initiated in Craig Gardner's, and minutes kept. Over a period of seven years this group made a series of decisions that changed the firm's ways of operating

[1] K. Bowen *Protestants in a Catholic State* (Dublin 1983) p 98.
[2] P. Kelleher 'Familism in Irish Capitalism in the 1950s' in *The Economic and Social Review* January 1987.

The partners in 1952 pictured at the annual staff dinner. (From left) Back row: W. S. Cunningham, G. W. O'Brien, D. McC. Watson, J. McCartney (Belfast); Front Row: J. Walker (Belfast), J. Russell, G. H. Tulloch, E. Sbott.

to something recognisably modern from the systems that had not significantly changed since John Mackie's time, thirty years before. The impetus came from the three men who had become partners together in 1944, Watson, Cunningham and O'Brien. Their first concern was to develop the quality of staff to meet the challenges of the new kind of work that the partners wanted to take on. This approach was not fortuitous: two of the three had been involved for some time in the development of professional education: O'Brien had been lecturing in Accountancy at UCD since 1935, and Watson had been chairman of the Dublin Society in 1950/1, and was a member of the 1956 subcommittee of the Institute appointed to consider the qualification examinations, and which recommended the five-part exam structure that was adopted in 1959. Another factor was a growing consciousness of the cost of staff time, and therefore of the need to make the most of it. Salaries had gone from 55 per cent of fees in 1948/9, to 60 per cent in 1952/3 and 1953/4, and reached a peak of 64 per cent in 1954/5. A jump in fees from the Sweep brought the ratio down below 60 per cent in 1957, and it fluctuated between 53 and 59 per cent up to 1968.

One of the very first decisions recorded in the committee's minutes was to appoint a staff manager. This had always been a partner's responsibility in the past, but with the increasing staff (there were by 1955 nine Dublin partners and twenty qualified Associates Not in Practice, not to mention the unqualified staff in the Sweep office, the secretarial, the tax and the audit juniors), discipline was seen as a rising problem. Partly this was caused by the very seasonal nature of the workload. In late summer there was very little work for the audit staff to do, and this naturally made it hard to impose tight time-keeping, and allowed bad habits to be built up.

Techniques of auditing at this time relied on heavy vouching and comprehensively checking postings and tots, not tasks to make the normal audit clerk hurry to work. A typical audit started, as it had done for decades, with the bank reconciliation, checking the cash book, the paid cheques, vouching up to four months of purchases, sales and wages. The actual accountancy task in producing the final profit and loss and balance sheet from the trial balance with numerous adjustments was an important part of the work.

On the other hand, clients such as J.C.M. Eason had not unreasonably complained, when his fee was raised, that he had spotted the clerks supposedly on his audit actually taking a coffee in Bewley's on their way between Dame Street and O'Connell Street. Discipline in the office was therefore to be tightened.

The job of Staff Manager was offered to J.F. MacDermott, who had qualified in 1952 in T. Geoghegan's, and had worked for some years in their Galway office. He had joined Craig Gardners in 1955. A group of partners was set up to liaise with MacDermott on staff matters. In 1959 he was asked to select suitable articled clerks to undertake development training in the expanding secretarial department. From this time phrases such as 'MacDermott to consider and put up suggestions' regularly recur in the minutes. MacDermott became the firm's first personnel partner in 1971.

MacDermott's major task was to control and allocate the audit staff. Some of these would be articled, by 1959 the allocation had gone up to four per partner, but others would be unqualified. In June 1959 there was a purge of six of the unqualified men, expressed in the blunt style of the minutes 'X — give him six months salary from 1 July and tell him that we find him unsuitable', though in the days before the development of employment legislation this was generous enough. MacDermott clearly managed to find replacements for the men who left, for by December 1959 he reported that there were enough audit staff for the heavy season of early 1960.

In the meantime the staff policy was advancing. In July 1958, the partners declared that 'the policy should be to build up good juniors as against recruitment of indifferent semi-seniors'. To this end there was a long campaign to increase the quality and exam success of the junior articled clerks. In a buyer's market the firm could pick and choose who to give articles to, and decided in January 1957 to insist on honours Leaving Certificate or the equivalent.

By Autumn 1963 there were 38 articled clerks, of whom 10 were graduates. Most clerks were introduced by a partner; the three clerks recorded as coming in by 'application' are all graduates. It was agreed that 'the appointment of articled clerks should be passed through the Committee of Partners who deal with appointments to staff. This will allow appraisal of our requirements on a proper basis with the opportunity of screening applicants to see that they have a good educational background. It is realised that personal approaches to individual partners will always be liable to be made, but a regular system will help very much in keeping the situation under control.' Like many of the innovations over these years, it seems surprising now that the previous partners had not regarded such arrangements as necessary. The firm was moving, like other commercial and industrial organisations, from the old personal ways to more 'business-like' modes of behaviour.

The passing of exams was another area which the partners began to be strict about. In July 1957 the minutes noted that 'any articled clerk who fails Intermediate Certificate twice should be liable to have his articles cancelled.'[3] When the exam system was changed after 1959, it was decided that candidates 'shall take all exams at the due date after completing requisite service', although there was some doubt as to whether the firm was within its rights in insisting on this. In April 1962 it was reported that 28 clerks were on exam leave, of whom 10 were second

---

[3] Under the Institute's regulations at the time, the Intermediate was the first examination of two required for qualification. It consisted of six papers.

timers, and it was confirmed that exam leave be refused thereafter for second attempts. In July 1963 the meeting recorded ominously that it would 'look into the position of articled clerks who have not made progress in their examinations'. In 1964 MacDermott circulated a note to staff reminding articled clerks that increments would only be given if the clerk was 'up to date with his examinations'. Broadly speaking clerks, whether three year (graduates) or five year, were expected to pass an exam every year.

By 1963 the number of unqualified seniors had dropped drastically. Of the 106 clerks there were 43 seniors, only 8 of whom were unqualified specialists in areas such as tax and management. There were 63 juniors, of whom 42 were in articles, 5 out of articles but still attempting exams and 16 others (including 10 students of ACCA). In December of that year MacDermott reports that he has to organise audit staff for 350 jobs over the next three months, and notes, somewhat plaintively, that he would 'appreciate advice beforehand of new work'.

In other ways the general management of the firm was brought up to date. The payment of premiums by articled clerks was abolished in 1957, and Saturday working in 1961.[4] In 1959 it was suggested that 'if proper time records were available, they could be linked with costing records.' A group was delegated to look into this, using information MacDermott had gleaned from a professional office in England. In 1960 a pension scheme for staff with more than ten years service was initiated — a VHI group had been set up a few years before. In 1961 audit clerks were told to report direct to jobs, rather than into the office first which continued only for Mondays. This innovation was felt to be risky, but in May the minutes reported with relief that the new system 'seems to be working satisfactorily — no adverse reports on time keeping.'

---

[4] The partners were careful to note, 'advise Stokes and Crowley as a matter of courtesy'.

In 1962 all the employees were put on salary scales, with the top seven men on a scale of £1,500 to £2,000 a year rising by £100 a year. The 1961/2 'pricing chart', a listing of the hourly charge-out rates of every member of staff (excluding partners), listed 190 staff, broken into eight categories. The top category contained six names, all earning more than £1,250, and charged out at 25/- to 30/- per hour. The biggest categories were E and F which contained nearly ninety names, with salaries up to £500, largely articled clerks, but also including long-serving staff in the Sweep and secretarial departments. These were charged out at 6/- or 10/- an hour. A few years later, by 1964/5, the staff had gone up by 12 per cent, and there were eight people on the top charge-out rate of 35/- to 42/-. At this time the Institute still issued recommended charging rates (expressed in guineas, in the old way) which in 1964 were: Managing

Table 2: Staff Charge-out rates 1964/5*

Grade	Number	Salary-range	Charge-out rate per hour
A	8	£1,500 +	35/- to 42/-
B	20	£1,251 — £1,500	30/-
C	34	£901 — £1,250	25/-
D	13	£701 — £900	20/-
E	21	£501 — £700	15/-
F	51	£301 — £500 & Typists	10/-
G	59	up to £300	6/
H	6	Comptometer and Machine Operators	12/6

*A full list of the staff in each of these grades makes up Appendix 4.

Clerks and principal assistants, 14 guineas per day of seven hours, senior assistants, 10 guineas, semi-senior assistants, 7 guineas, and juniors 3 to 5 guineas.

In 1963 the question of using a computer was raised, and in 1964 the provision of pensions for the younger partners was under serious discussion for the first time.

At the same time as the campaign to improve the quality of the staff was going on, the firm was consciously looking for development outside the sphere of audit. In 1958 the constituents of fees were recorded in the private ledger for the first time, showing that the total fee income was £138,000, of which 69 per cent was from audit (which included liquidation fees and the Sweep). The audit department before the war certainly contributed a very much larger per cent of the fees, though analysed figures do not survive. It is likely that the partners' awareness of the changing relationships between the departments led to a desire to record what was happening in more detail than had previously been necessary. Tax work contributed 7 per cent, secretarial and 'special' work 12 per cent each. There were £2,440 of directors' fees.

The secretarial department underwent significant change in the 1950s. This department had traditionally provided a largely clerical service. Thus when Unidare went public in the 1950s, thousands of prospectuses had to be despatched, applications processed, and then there was the continuing work of organising the share register (an active share might require a hundred or more transfers a month, particularly immediately after the launch), calculating and despatching interim and final dividends, and despatching the annual reports, proxy vote forms and so on. During the 1950s tax and company law legislation enabled George Coleman and others to develop a different technical expertise in the secretarial department. Coleman was a TCD graduate with various academic distinctions who had taken articles and qualified after joining the secretarial department. He was made a partner in 1957. Developments in British corporate reporting after their 1948 Act gradually led to several large Irish companies adopting the new standards for profit and loss reporting and consolidated accounts. This considerably increased the complexity and sophistication of the audit report from the simple and uncommunicative norms of the 1908 Act. A much greater knowledge and understanding of company law became important. By 1959 it was a policy to give selected articled clerks three months' training in the department. Coleman was the firm's specialist in these matters; it was he for instance who was asked to consider in 1962 what submission, if any, the firm should make on the new Companies Bill.

The implications of Estate Duty on companies that were, as we have seen, largely dominated by family holdings, prompted the firm to devise tax-effective corporate packages, which would minimise the effects of the death of a major shareholder. Many companies had incorporated themselves in the nineteenth century specifically to avoid the destructive effects of the death of one of the partners; now the fiscal consequences of the death of a major shareholder had to be guarded against. One device was the use of investment companies, of which the firm controlled several hundred at one point. In 1963 the partners' meeting minutes record 'specialist audit section required for investment trusts — attempt to train two or three good men in this.' Later legislation rendered these companies less effective, and they fell out of use.

The second major development at this time was the setting up of the management consultancy service. Since the war it had been clear that this was a service that the accountancy profession as a whole were reluctant to provide. Just as in the nineteenth century solicitors had allowed the development of the accountancy profession out of what could so easily have been their territory, accountants did the same for management consultants in the twentieth. In both cases a rather rigid view of the business the profession was in, caused an opportunity to be missed, though accountants subsequently recovered at least some of the territory lost by them.

In Britain and America the experience of running manufacturing concerns under pressure during the war had led to the wider knowledge of work study, organisation and methods and other descendants of F. Taylor's 'scientific management' techniques for improving shop-floor productivity. Statistical quality control techniques, pioneered in the Bell laboratories in America, were also in the air, as were costing techniques. The chartered profession remained aloof from all of this for a long time.

In the 1950s the Craig Gardner partners began to look into the area. Their first step was to appoint a non-accountant from a firm called Production Engineering to develop a management service. In January 1957 the partners' meeting reported that it was 'difficult to see at this stage how we can detail a senior man whole time to this type of work.' Staff was taken from the general audit body as and when necessary, and in November 1958 MacDermott complained that the section was affecting the availability of certain staff. The next step, agreed in February 1959, was to 'indicate the prospect of a partnership' to Noel MacMahon, who had qualified in 1954, 'if he makes himself fully competent to deal with cost consultancy management and modern machine accountancy. If he agrees we should approach Price Waterhouse and ask them whether they would take him for 6 months on to their staff in a similar department.' The partners were urged to try to sell these new services to clients.

MacMahon went to Price Waterhouse in 1960, and on his return he was made a partner. In May 1962 he submitted a memorandum to his colleagues on how he saw the management services area developing. The purpose of the memo 'is to indicate in general terms the scope of the work which, at this stage, we should be prepared to undertake.' Although this was the cutting edge of thought on the subject in the firm at the time, what strikes one now is the extreme caution of the approach.

The focus of the service is very much the accounts department of the client company, rather than the company as a whole. Four areas are indicated as suitable; these being systems of accounting, clerical methods, management accounting and advice on administrative organisation. The first area was straightforward: 'as Accountants we should be prepared to investigate and to advise on accounting systems generally.' This was to include the setting up of accounting records, problems associated with prompt preparation of annual accounts, and general accounting problems such as stock valuation, depreciation, retail stock control and the classification and coding of accounts.

Secondly, the writer felt that 'we are competent to advise on clerical methods and the paperwork associated with accounting procedures, for example stores recording procedures, buying office records, sales office records . . . We would be prepared to recommend the use of mechanised systems' such as aided manual systems, pegboards, posting boards, keyboard machines, copying and reproducing machines and general information on punched card machines. Detailed advice on the use of computers or punched card equipment is specifically ruled out.

The new section could also undertake to advise on the type and form of accounting and statistical information which should be provided for management, and finally on the organisational problems caused by the improvement of any accounting system, though only to the extent that they were related to accounting requirements. 'We should not, however, comment on the competence of individuals in particular posts, except for accounting personnel.' Specifically ruled out were production efficiency surveys, time study, rate setting and job evaluation, market research, sales policies and operational research.

The new section is envisaged more as providing an added service to audit clients, rather than as a business-getter in its own right. The idea that management services might be presented as a carrot to tempt new audit clients was not envisaged: 'up to now the work we have undertaken has been for existing clients of the firm. It is unlikely that this pattern will change to any great extent. However in cases where we are asked to carry out work for "non-clients", we should be careful to seek the prior approval of the auditors of the firm concerned.'

Even audit work, for long the staple activity of the company, was subject to development during this time. By the end of the 1950s it was clear that as companies became larger, and the amount of accounts paper grew, some of the techniques used in very large audits such as CIE could usefully be made more general. By November 1960 work on a specimen set of working papers was well advanced. In May 1962 the partners agreed that Noel MacMahon should 'consider audit procedures in the light of modern methods.' MacMahon was not long back from his period with Price Waterhouse in London, and had been impressed there by the work that Stan Duncan, later senior partner of Price Waterhouse, had been carrying out in standardising audit working papers. In 1963 MacMahon drafted a booklet on the audit implications of the new Companies Act.

Perhaps the area of work least affected by development at this time was that of insolvency, for which Craig Gardner had a well-established reputation. In the early 1950s William Cunningham was appointed liquidator in a case which eventually went to court, where the principle was established that the liquidator's costs took precedence even over preferential creditors, a point that had been in some doubt since the 1908 Companies Act. The case involved the bankruptcy of a company called the Redbreast Preserving Company, which was run by an Dublin character known as 'Mincemeat Joe' Griffin, from his principal product. Griffin's fame arose from his race-horses, with which he won at least two Grand Nationals; his victories were accompanied by great publicity and expensive parties, including on one occasion the introduction of the winning horse into the ballroom of the Gresham Hotel.

One of the most extraordinary liquidations the firm was ever involved in was that of Shanahan's Stamp Auctions Ltd, which broke in 1959. The company centred round the outlandish figure of Dr Paul Singer, an Austrian, who had already been involved in the collapse of a small company

1940-1963 DUBLIN FEES & PARTNERS % OF FEES

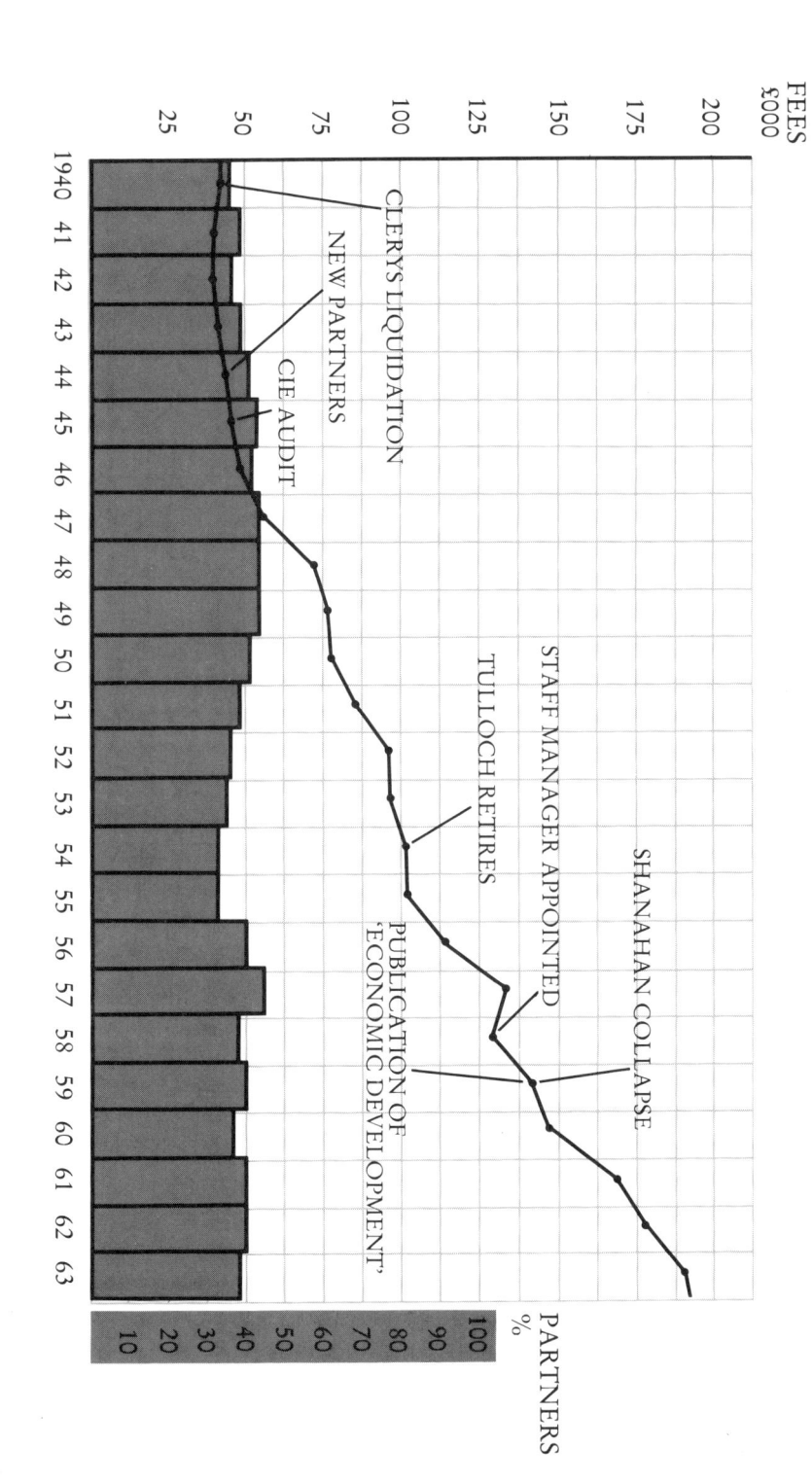

in London. He visited Ireland and decided to capitalise on his hobby of stamp collecting. In 1954 he approached a small family auctioneering company in Dun Laoghaire called Shanahans, and together they set up the stamp auction company, with a capital of £200. With this money Singer went to London and purchased a few small collections of stamps. These were sold at auction for a small profit.

The next step was to drum up more custom, which Singer did through a publication called *Green I.S.L.E. Philately*, gradually making wilder and wilder promises about the profitability of stamps as investments. Eventually he was promising to deliver 'between 20 and 100 per cent profit on the capital invested' within four months, and on investments as small as £10. The money was to enable Singer to buy stamps in various international markets, where he claimed he knew how to buy stamps cheap. They would then be sold at a profit from the auction rooms in Dún Laoghaire. His advertising contained the classic conman's pitch: 'if your problem is a small capital which you want to invest with absolute security, but with an unusually large return, then stamps are the solution', and money poured in. There was a lot of American money, and even some from Australia, but the bulk came from Europe, especially Ireland, Britain and Italy.

By 1958 Singer was receiving money at the rate of £5.25m a year. This enormous flow of money, bolstered by his flair for publicity, gave him a serious problem — where was he to find a matching flow of stamps, and where was he to find the buyers, at a profit, of these stamps? However, his frequent trips abroad seemed to be going well,[5] and the fortnightly auctions were well attended (though it was noted that there were very few room bids). Until the final inevitable collapse,

---

[5] 'Singer used to arrange for most of the ninety men and girls of his staff to greet him at the airport, and to sing from the balconies as the passengers disembarked *For he's a jolly good fellow*.' S. Brady *Doctor of Millions* (Tralee 1965) p 30.

no one actually lost money, though the auditors continually pointed out their suspicions of the overvaluation of stock.

Singer kept up the pace by wildly overvaluing in the catalogue the stamps he bought from abroad, and then taking bids off the wall at the auction, and reporting to the investors profitable sales that never took place. Later evidence revealed that the auctions were run at bewildering speed — on one occasion 630 lots were disposed of at a rate of more than four a minute. With a certain humour he invented names for his fictitious purchasers, including a 'Mr Zombie', whose ledger card revealed that he owed the company £235,000 for stamps supposedly bought at the auctions. Investors were paid with later income. Eventually the bubble burst, as it had to.

On 9 May 1959 the firm suffered a robbery of one of Singer's recent purchases, the Lombardo-Venezia collection. This was variously valued at anything from £100,000 to £460,000. It was not insured. Rumours had begun circulating in Dublin about Singer's operation, and stamp experts in London had long looked askance at the valuations in Shanahan's catalogues. The robbery gave the newspapers a chance to cover the story in detail, and the result was something of a panic as the Dún Laoghaire offices were besieged by people wanting their money back. This was the final straw. The sale that was to have featured the stolen stamps was cancelled, and the forthcoming sale of an even more famous collection was announced. But it wasn't enough. On Monday 25 May Arthur Cox & Co. announced that the firm was going into liquidation, and that the shareholders had appointed Mr G.W. O'Brien FCA of Messrs Craig Gardner & Co. as the liquidator.

That morning O'Brien attended the offices in Dún Laoghaire with John Milliken, who was a keen philatelist. Des Hally recalls how they were shown up to Singer's large office, with its large desk and chair. Singer got up to greet the liquidator and his staff in his usual extravagant way, and began showing them the office: by the time he turned round, O'Brien was seated behind the desk, in his chair. It was as neat a demonstration of the new power relationship as could be imagined, and one that Singer would instantly understand. The news of the liquidation did not appease the investors' fears, and rightly so, for O'Brien quickly discovered that there were nothing like enough assets to meet the liabilities, and so the members' liquidation could not be continued. He applied to the Court and after a hearing he was appointed official Liquidator by the Court.

The firm organised an auction of the stamps, and later arranged for a British stamp expert, Robson Lowe, to inspect and catalogue those remaining. In the meantime Singer and his fellow-directors had been arrested for fraud. After long delays, and bitter acccusations in the Dáil of incompetence on the part of the authorities, Singer was brought to trial. He and his counsel managed to make such confusions about the technical impossibility of proof that specific moneys had been used to pay specific dividends that he was acquitted of fraud, and he left the country, leaving the Irish public poorer by some £1m. It was a most complex liquidation. Mr Justice Budd had decided that because of the way the Shanahan system operated, each group of persons involved in a syndicate was a different class of creditor; in the end there were some 45 classes, each of which received different dividends, depending on the success of the sales of the stamps earmarked to them. In all there were over eleven thousand creditors, each of whom had to be paid amounts differing by their investment and by the dividend. Computers were heavily used to calculate the amounts and print out the cheques, the court having made a special order withdrawing the rule that in a court liquidation all cheques had to be personally signed by the Liquidator and the Examiner to the High Court. The final dividend was paid in 1968, nine years after the collapse, and the total fee was a record for the time of £55,000.

By 1964 the firm had put in train many of the internal changes needed to face what Dr Howard Robinson calls 'the period of mergers'. It had begun to shed the one-dimensional aspect — relying too heavily on an established position in audit — that had led to the practice losing ground. In general, it was becoming clear that 'the width of knowledge required to conduct an accountancy practice, other than one of the most limited scope, became greater than the ordinary individual accountant could absorb. The need for practising accountants to amalgamate into larger groups, which was beginning to be apparent in 1963, became more pressing...'.[6] How the firm faced this challenge is the subject of the next and final chapter of the firm's history up to 1968.

---

[6] H. Robinson *A History of Accountants in Ireland* 2nd edn (Dublin 1983) p 221.

CHAPTER 9

THE MODERN FIRM

The firm was by 1964 very far towards what it has now become. Turnover was £256,000, two and a half times what it had been ten years before. Discounting for inflation, this represented a 70 per cent real increase in the decade. Although this was in fact statistically less impressive than the growth from a turnover of £48,000 to £101,000, achieved between 1945 and 1954, the firm was clearly participating in the great surge forward that the Irish economy enjoyed after 1958. The policy changes that caused this surge were based on the phasing-out of protection against imports, the encouragement of exporting industries, and the welcoming of foreign capital, particularly if it led to exports. In general the country's businesses were being asked to look to the outside world for the first time since 1932.

The effect of these policies on the country was marked, most notably in emigration: 'the Irish population, having declined with few interruptions since the Famine, at first stabilised and then started to increase in the early sixties.'[1] The Second Vatican Council, the election of President Kennedy, the introduction of national television in December 1961, were other factors that changed the atmosphere in the country to a new openness and outward-lookingness. No less important was the increased importance of trade in the Irish economy: exports rose from 25 per cent of GNP in 1960 to 51 per cent in 1985. Manufacturing exports rose 19 per cent in the 1960s, largely as a result of overseas export-oriented investors: 'new green-field plants were set up all over the country ... by 1966 these enterprises accounted for 50 per cent of Irish manufacturing exports ... success in the export development drive meant that Ireland was able to sustain

---

[1] D. McAleese 'The Changing Economic Environment' in F.S.L. Lyons (ed.) *Bicentenary Essays, Bank of Ireland 1783-1983* (Dublin 1983) p 152.

a growth of 6 per cent annually in industrial output over the period 1961-73.'[2]

Ireland was opening up in other ways too. The gradual economic integration of western Europe, as Ireland became part of the Anglo-Irish free trade area, EFTA and finally the EEC, led people increasingly to compare Ireland's progress in matters such as education with western European standards. In 1963, after some heart searching, the Institute joined the Union Européenne des Experts Comptables Economique et Financier (or UEC) which had been formed in 1951. Accountancy standards that had previously been relevant mainly to Britain and America began to be significant in Ireland. Several companies had in fact anticipated the terms of the 1963 Companies Act in their annual reports, and by 1967 it was clear that the revelations of the GEC/AEI takeover in Britain were going to impinge strongly. The auditors of AEI had approved a forecast profit of £14m in 1967, but after the take-over, the actual figures showed a loss of £4.5m. It was announced that most of the difference arose out of 'adjustments which remain matters substantially of judgement.' The confusion and dismay that this caused among the investing public speeded the formation by the accountancy bodies of the Accounting Standards Steering Committee, established by the three Institutes in these islands, on which Craig Gardner partner W.B. Lyster was the first Irish representative.

Economic development obviously meant more business for the profession. In 1964 just over 1,000 new companies were registered in Ireland, and by 1970 over 2,000 a year were starting. Admittedly most of these companies were still small — half of them had a nominal capital of less than £5,000, and the average paid-up capital of all companies on the register was just £20,000. However with this opening of

[2] McAleese p 154.

the market it is not surprising that by the end of the decade, Craig Gardner's fee income had gone up to £571,000 by 1969, an increase in real terms of nearly 80 per cent in five years.

However the strength of international corporations in the economy represented a potential threat to the continuation of this growth. The trend in the accountancy profession in Britain since the war had been for audit work of large quoted companies to be spread among fewer and fewer firms, usually because of take-overs and mergers among the companies. Between 1948 and 1978 the total number of public companies quoted on the London Stock Exchange dropped nearly 50 per cent, to less than three thousand. Over the same period accountancy firms with any quoted clients fell 64 per cent.[3] The accountancy profession was rapidly polarising into the very large firms, able to offer a widely diversified service, and the very small, offering an extremely personal service.

This trend was echoed to some extent in Ireland, perhaps first in the banking sector. In 1958 the Bank of Ireland acquired the capital of the Hibernian Bank and in 1966 the National Bank. Later that year the Allied Irish Bank group was set up by the fusion of the Munster and Leinster, the Provincial and the Royal. Craig Gardner had been joint auditors of the Bank of Ireland since the mid 1960s with Deloittes, and now took over the audit of two other banks. In international terms, Craig Gardner was not a large firm. On the other hand it was the biggest firm in Ireland, and therefore attractive to potential partners overseas whose clients had subsidiaries in Ireland.

In 1963 the minutes of the partners' meetings record an approach by the head of the London firm Cooper Brothers, Sir Henry Benson, whom Robinson describes as 'the most dynamic British accountant of his time', but

---

[3] E. Jones *Accountancy and the British Economy 1840-1980* (London 1981) p 226.

nothing came of it. In 1965 Cooper Brothers combined with the Belfast partnership of Rawlinson, Allen & White, and in 1968 with three medium-sized Dublin firms, Kean's, Kevan's and Peterson Morrison. By 1973 this firm had become Coopers and Lybrand.[4] Various other feelers were put out, offering different degrees of integration. The most detailed proposal was offered by the senior partner of a London firm. This firm had already been, as the minutes of the meeting with him recorded

> forced to adapt their organisation so that they would be in a position to provide services in all parts of the world, and that they were unwilling to do this by opening subsidiary offices in the various countries ... [they] have already set up firms in conjunction with local accountants in various countries in Europe and Africa and in Australia, and would very much like to do so in Ireland with ourselves.
>
> The proposal is that a partnership should be set up here the name of which would incorporate in some way the names of the partners. This firm would undertake any work in Ireland passed on to it by their associated firms in other countries, and would certify statements as required in its own name. The work would in fact be carried out by Craig Gardner for the proposed firm. Of the fees received 90 per cent would be retained by Craig Gardner, 2½ per cent would be paid to the firm introducing the work, 2½ per cent to the partners of the proposed firm, and 5 per cent would be retained by the latter for its own purposes.

[4] H. Robinson *A History of Accountants in Ireland* 2nd edn (Dublin 1983) p 236.

In the event nothing came of this approach either. One reason was that Craig Gardner was by this time receiving quite a lot of work from cross-Channel firms, and it was felt that if the firm linked with one particular firm, it would damage contacts with the others. Negotiations were progressing, however, with Price Waterhouse. They had been initiated on an informal basis by Charles Nicholson, a Price Waterhouse partner who had been articled in Craig Gardner's from 1929 to 1934. The first point of contact was the Belfast office, which had amalgamated in 1967 with the local firm Ashworth Rowan. The new firm separated from Craig Gardner's, leaving only four partners, who were on a nominal salary, with the Dublin firm. In 1968 the combined firm became the Price Waterhouse correspondents in Belfast.

Negotiations with the Dublin office were however delayed for some time by the outbreak of the disturbances in the North, which had got increasingly violent in 1970 (the Arms Trial was in September of that year). Because feeling was running so high, it was not considered a suitable time to make a public announcement of a link with a firm of London accountants. In 1971, however, it was announced that Nicholson and another Price Waterhouse partner would become partners in the firm, which would henceforth practise under the name of Price Waterhouse as well as Craig Gardner. A similar arrangement was enacted in the north. The four northern partners ceased at this time to be also partners in the Dublin firm.

While this was going on, the internal structures of the firm were being changed to cope with the new business and the fact that there were now over two hundred employees. The recruitment of specialists in the management, tax and secretarial areas, who often had no accountancy qualification, gradually changed the character of the firm. The accountancy training, the audit experience and the Institute's exams ceased to be a common bond. George Coleman had qualified while in the secretarial department, but others in his position felt less need to do so. One aspect of the development of the firm put in hand by this time was the change in the status of the partners. The career opportunities for good qualified accountants were increasing all the time, especially in industry. Of the twenty qualified Associates Not in Practice in the firm in 1955, only eight were still with the firm ten years later, two of whom were partners. Of the rest, two had gone to Britain, two into state-sponsored bodies and the rest into various industries. None had joined other accountancy firms in Ireland.

The policy of carefully selecting and developing good juniors would be useless if they were at once poached by industry when they qualified. It was therefore necessary to offer partnerships more readily to suitable men. Tied up with this was the problem of the creation of staff managers. Specifically the partners had some trouble deciding whether they wanted or needed a layer organising the flow of audit work between them and the senior clerks. And if they did, should the manager-grade be seen as a stepping stone to partnership, or as a career for those who would never be partners? The question was raised in the partners' meeting in 1960, when MacDermott was to organise a scheme on agreed lines, enlisting the cooperation of the seniors and the management section. A few months later the idea was regarded less positively. It was felt that 'it is possible to deal with administrative aspects [of the audit programme] without managers — supervising clerks to deal with completion of jobs.' By June 1965 it was finally decided to 'create a manager class' as the minutes put it. Later the whole function of planning the flow of audit work was put on a different basis, with the creation of an Audit Planning function run by two partners.

The creation of new partners was done gradually, but in the long run did have the effect of diluting the close-knit nature of the partnership. In December 1963 the minutes of the partners' meeting record that four men were considered as potential partners, one of whom had not even qualified yet.

PARTNERS LENGTH OF SERVICE 1866-1968

	1860	70	80	90	1900	10	20	30	40	50	60	70

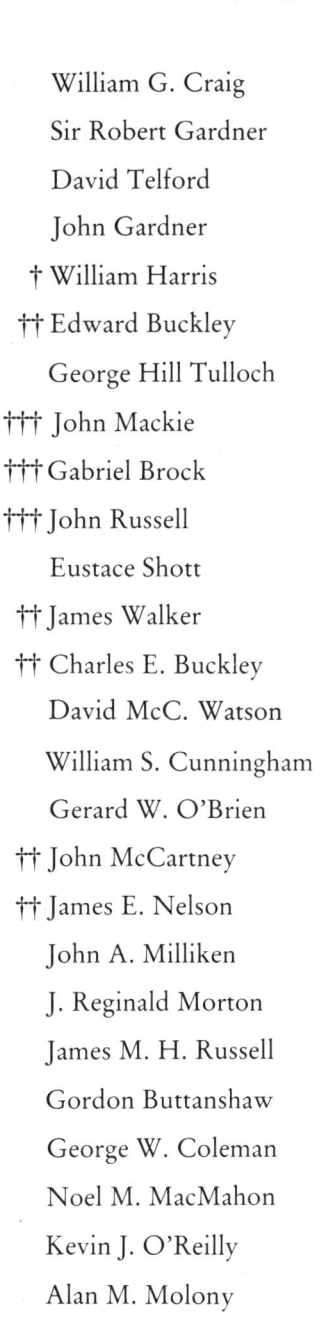

- William G. Craig
- Sir Robert Gardner
- David Telford
- John Gardner
- † William Harris
- †† Edward Buckley
- George Hill Tulloch
- ††† John Mackie
- ††† Gabriel Brock
- ††† John Russell
- Eustace Shott
- †† James Walker
- †† Charles E. Buckley
- David McC. Watson
- William S. Cunningham
- Gerard W. O'Brien
- †† John McCartney
- †† James E. Nelson
- John A. Milliken
- J. Reginald Morton
- James M. H. Russell
- Gordon Buttanshaw
- George W. Coleman
- Noel M. MacMahon
- Kevin J. O'Reilly
- Alan M. Molony
- W. Bruce Lyster

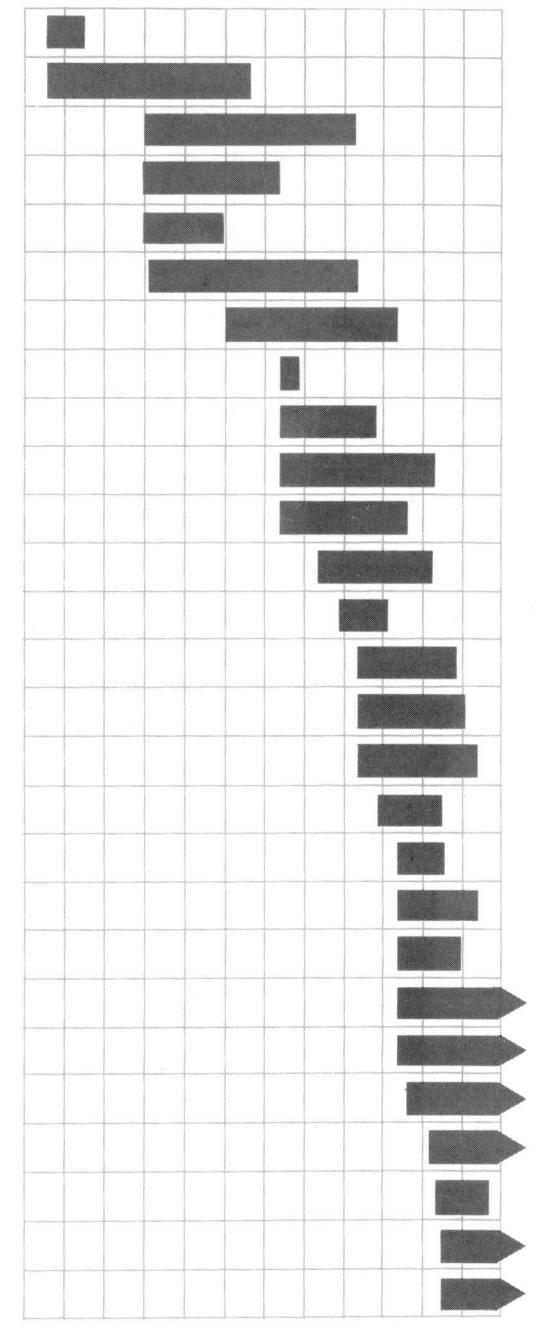

† *London based 1904-1910*   †† *Belfast based*   ††† *Mackie Amalgamation*

The structure of income was still dominated by audit fees, but not so much as for the larger audit-based firms in Britain. Despite the rapid growth in overall income, the ratios of contribution of the various divisions remained broadly stable over the 1960s. Craig Gardner's audit fee figure, which included liquidation fees and also the Sweep, was 59 per cent of total income. Tax work stood in 1962/3 at 6½ per cent of total fees, just less than it had been in 1958/9, though the actual receipts were 43 per cent more than five years previously. The real growth in this department was to come after 1973, with major investment flows into the country and when the coalition government began a substantial tax reform package, and at the same time increased the number and complexity of tax-based industrial incentives. The tax department was to treble in size as a result of these developments. In 1962/3 Craig Gardner's 'special' work reached a high of 22 per cent; the following year it fell to 14 per cent, and then picked up again to 20 per cent. By 1964, after the passing of the Companies Act, the secretarial department's fees had reached £37,000, more than double what they had been in 1958. For the year ended April 1969, the year of the move of office to Ballsbridge, the ratios were: audit 60 per cent, special 20 per cent, secretarial 14 per cent and tax 6 per cent.[5]

The death of Joe MacGrath in 1965 brought back memories of the great days of the Sweep in the 1930s, when it represented 30 per cent of the firm's income; by 1959/60 it was less than 15 per cent, and by 1968/9 less than 10 per cent. The Sweep itself was increasingly competing with national lotteries in other countries, many of whom paid out a higher percentage of the takings in prizes. One great source of competition, the British football pools, on the other hand, paid out considerably less — 38 per cent as against 55 per cent. At the end the Sweeps

---

[5] In 1987 the top five British firms reported their income proportions as: audit 57 per cent, tax 19 per cent, management consultancy 17 per cent and insolvency 7 per cent, *The Accountant* June 1987.

were run four times a year, and the firm's staff involved were under pressure to keep up with the prize payments. The final days of the Sweep were signalled in the mid 1970s, when various states in America, which was by then contributing 80 per cent of the cash, began their own lotteries.

The growth in staff that was required to service the new business made the old offices in Dame Street more and more crowded. Since 1955 various makeshifts had been adopted to eke out the space. The old board-room that Gardner and Telford had occupied in their turn was divided into two; then the ground floor of 40/41 became available and was used for audit managers and some of the senior staff. The ground floor of No. 38, which had been a private bank (Farrow's, long since gone, though their name survived in the terrazzo entrance hall) was turned into the Sweepstake office. By December 1964 the partners' meeting records a discussion under the heading 'Premises'. A sub-committee was working on this, a key question being — 'how far should we go out?'. A limiting factor was said to be the secretarial department's relationship with the Stock Exchange. Later that month, the meeting agreed that no more than 20,000 sq. ft should be required.

Eventually, with the help of long-time client G. & T. Crampton, the firm was able to acquire two houses in Ballsbridge. By coincidence one of these had been the residence of Thomas Geoghegan, an ex-president of the Institute and auditor among other companies of the first semi-state body, the Agricultural Credit Corporation, whose firm was later to become part of Reynolds McCarron. The two houses were demolished and after certain alterations were made to the drainage, the building of Gardner House, Ballsbridge, began. It was finished in September 1968, and the move to the new premises was made immediately.[6]

---

[6] These offices now house the Institute of Chartered Accountants in Ireland which took over the premises when the firm moved again in 1984.

Gardner House in Ballsbridge, Trinity Chambers' successor, by Ruth Brandt. The firm's headquarters from 1968 to 1984, following which it became the offices for the Institute of Chartered Accountants in Ireland.

After 102 years in the same building, the move naturally unearthed many treasures, including, in an old press, the certificate of qualification of David Mack, an old Craig Gardner man who had been General Manager of the Royal Bank, and who had introduced William Cunningham to the firm in 1927. Moving house is always troublesome, and naturally all sorts of immediate inconveniences arose, one at least of which would now not arise. David Watson, who had been President of the Institute in 1959/60, felt that it was necessary to check with the Institute about announcing the move. The Council decided that an announcement of the change of address would amount to advertising, and so none was made. Eighty years after the issue of professional advertising had been settled by the brand-new Institute, Robert Gardner's firm policy on the subject had come home to roost.

By the end of 1968 the firm was settled into its new home, and in common with other service industries enjoying a growth in fee income comfortably faster than the Irish economy as a whole. At the time, as Gerard O'Brien put it, 'it was considered that we had then ample accommodation for some considerable time to come.' This view of the future development of the firm proved to be quite wrong: growth was continuous over the next twenty years. David Watson was senior partner, handing over in 1969 to William Cunningham. Of the three young partners admitted together in 1944, whose links with the firm went back to the very different days of 1927, Watson was the first to become senior partner. Gerard O'Brien was by this time Professor of Accountancy in UCD, a post he held until 1971, when he in turn became senior partner a position he held until his own retirement in 1974. This marked the end of an era in the firm's history, and thereafter it was felt that the senior partner should be elected rather than achieve his eminence automatically. The change also recognised that in a firm employing (by then) over 400 people and providing a very diverse range of services, the nature of the responsibilities of the senior partner had changed considerably.

Conclusion

Professional accountancy practice has long been identified in the public mind with auditing, and to a lesser extent with taxation work. Yet it is clear from the history of Craig Gardner, that for barely half of the firm's long history was auditing as such the dominant interest of the firm, and the tax department was very small until the 1970s. The firm started by checking the accounts of land agents, then majored on insolvency for several decades before auditing (which was usually in truth as much accountancy, even book keeping, as auditing) became at the beginning of this century the power-house of the firm.

Four elements in the development of a professional firm are felt as daily pressures; as their force varies, so does the growth of the firm. At different times in the history of a firm one factor or another becomes important over the others. The four factors are: the acquisition of new business; the technical and professional skills deployed; the internal administrative arrangements; and the fees paid. Each of these factors impinges on the others. The kind of fees available for certain types of work affects the partners' decisions to develop professional skills in that direction and vice versa — George Coleman's development of the secretarial department is a classic case. The internal arrangements, including the ease with which promotion comes to ambitious qualified men, can significantly affect development.

Above all these factors lies a further overriding consideration: that of the current understanding of the role and duties of a professional accountant. The history of Craig Gardner teems with examples of how this changes. In the early 1900s the partners invested heavily in their clients' new issues; they freely took directorships, a practice that was frowned on thirty years later; and they gave blunt, detailed and apparently unbespoken advice to their clients on how they should run their businesses. On the other hand they would have regarded advertising, or proposing for work, as quite beneath the dignity of the professional man.

The concept of the profession was a Victorian invention, and some of the notions of that era which still clung in 1968 (as witness the Institute's unwillingness to allow the firm to announce its change of address) have been shed. The pressures of increasing development in recent years, both inside the firm, which grew from two hundred employees in the Republic of Ireland in 1968 at the time of the move, to four hundred in 1974 and six hundred in 1987,[7] and in the profession as a whole have led to many of these notions being challenged. The results of the challenge however will be for the historian of the firm's next hundred years to record.

---

[7] Part of this growth was of course by amalgamation with the old firms of Atkins Chirnside in Cork 1973, and with Coffey Gubbins of Limerick in 1975 and Metcalfe Lilburn Enright, also of Limerick, in 1976.

Appendix I

CRAIG GARDNER PARTNERS 1866-1987

William G. Craig	1866 – 1875	Alan M. Molony	1965 to date
Sir Robert Gardner	1866 – 1917	W. Bruce Lyster	1965 to date
David Telford	1890 – 1943	George E. Egar	1969 to date
John Gardner	1890 – 1924	Michael Manley	1969 – 1982
William Harris	1890 – 1903	D. Brendan Gallagher	1971 to date
Edward Buckley	1901 – 1944	John F. MacDermott	1971 – 1978
George Hill Tulloch	1910 – 1954	Frank E. Belton	1972 to date
*John Mackie[1]	1924 – 1929	William M. McCann	1972 to date
*Gabriel Brock[1]	1924 – 1949	Joe O'Broin	1972 to date
*John Russell[1]	1924 – 1964	*Paddy J. Blanc[2]	1973 – 1985
Eustace Shott	1924 – 1957	*Barclay P. Clibborn[2]	1973 – 1976
James Walker	1934 – 1963	*John A. O'Connell[2]	1973 – 1978
Charles E. Buckley	1939 – 1952	*Derry O'Neill[2]	1973 to date
David McC Watson	1944 – 1969	*Anthony Thornton[2]	1973 to date
William Cunningham	1944 – 1971	Thomas E. Meehan	1974 to date
Gerard W. O'Brien	1944 – 1974	D. Vincent O'Leary	1974 – 1986
John McCartney	1949 – 1967	*P. Oliver Coffey[3]	1975 – 1984
James E. Nelson	1954 – 1967	*Seamus A. Gubbins[3]	1975 to date
John A. Milliken	1954 – 1974	*Patrick A. Kevans[3]	1975 to date
J. Reginald Morton	1954 – 1970	*Tom J. O'Higgins[3]	1975 to date
James M. H. Russell	1954 – 1980	John D. Hourihane	1975 to date
Gordon Buttanshaw	1954 – 1983	E. John Bourke	1976 to date
George W. Coleman	1957 – 1984	Sean Cleary	1976 to date
Noel M. MacMahon	1962 to date	John Blake Dillon	1976 to date
Kevin J. O'Reilly	1964 – 1978	*P. Gerard Boland[4]	1976 to date

*Admitted to partnership in Craig Gardner on its amalgamation with: 1. Mackie & Co. in 1924; 2. Atkins, Chirnside & Co. in 1973; 3. Coffey, Gubbins & Co. in 1975; and 4. Metcalf, Lilburn, Enright & Co. in 1976.

The firm has given seven presidents to the Institute of Chartered Accountants in Ireland including Sir Robert Gardner, the first president at the Institute's formation in 1888 and also David Telford; John Mackie; Gabriel Brock; James Walker; David Watson and Noel MacMahon; and to University College, Dublin, the first Professor of Accountancy, Gerard O'Brien.

*Dermot FitzGerald[4]	1976 to date	Tom Grace	1983 to date
*Stewart Lilburn[4]	1976 – 1979	Willie McAteer	1983 to date
*Gordon A. Milne[4]	1976 to date	Donal O'Connor	1983 to date
*G. Don Milne[4]	1976 – 1979	Anthony J. Weldon	1983 to date
*W. Trevor Morrow[4]	1976 to date	Peter G. Kelly	1983 to date
John Blake	1979 to date	John M. Kelly	1986 to date
Tadhg O'Donoghue	1979 to date	Declan McKeon	1986 to date
David R. Algeo	1980 to date	Marie O'Connor	1986 to date
David L. Devlin	1980 to date	Michael O'Neill	1986 to date
F. Bryan Evans	1980 to date	George Reddin	1986 to date
Jimmy O'Sullivan	1980 to date	Paul Cummins	1987 to date
W. Roy Hanan	1981 to date	Robert W. Semple	1987 to date
Peter Lacy	1981 to date	Aidan Walsh	1987 to date
Michael Long	1981 to date	Kevin Warren	1987 to date
Denis Cremins	1982 to date		

Appendix 2

CLIENTS IN THE LATE 1890s

Exors. H. M. Anretell-Jones
Ahenny Dairy Co. Ltd.
Anderson & McAuly
Arnott & Co. Ltd.
Armstrong & Co.
Allman & Co.
Allman, Dowden & Co.
Arklow Harbour
    Commissioners
Austin & Co.
Col. Alexander

Bagots Hutton & Co. Ltd.
Ballinrobe & Claremorris
    Light Railway
Sir Hy. Grattan Bellew
Brooks Thomas & Co. Ltd.
Bewley & Draper Ltd.
J. & G. Boyd Ltd.
Belfast Banking Co. Ltd.
Baker Wardell & Co.
E. & J. Burke Ltd.
Blessington & Poulaphucca
    Steam Tramways
Robert L. Brown
J. Brewster
Daniel D. Bulger
Baldoyle Race Company
Boileau & Boyd
Wm. Burke Decd.

Castlebellingham &
    Drogheda Breweries
E. Cannon & Sons Ltd.
City of Dublin Hospital
Cannock & Co. Ltd.
T. & J. Connick & Co.
P. J. Carroll & Co.
Cavan & Leitrim Light
    Railways Co.
Crowe Wilson & Co. Ltd.

Clarence Hotel Co. Ltd.
Victor Coates & Co.
Convoy Woollen Co. Ltd.
Chase & Co.
Clery & Co.
J. & G. Campbell
J. F. Corscaden Decd.
Connell Bros.
Adm. of Thos. W. Coster
Crown Hotel
Cherry & Smalldridge Ltd.
G. D. Christie & Co.
Coombe Hospital
City of Dublin Nursing
    Institution Ltd.
N. Carolan & Co.

W. Drummond & Sons Ltd.
Dublin United Tramways
    Co. Ltd.
Dublin & Lucan Steam
    Tramways Co.
Dublin & Wicklow Manure
    Co.
Dublin Distillers Co. Ltd.
Thos. Dockrell Sons &
    Co. Ltd.
Dublin & Suburban Work-
    mens Dwellings
    Co. Ltd.
Duncan Alderdice & Co.
Davis Strangman & Co. Ltd.
Dundalk Advertising Co.
D'Arcy & Son
Dundalk Gas Co. Ltd.
Dundalk & Newry Steam
    Packet Co.
Dundalk Race Co. Ltd.
Drogheda Chemical
    Manure Co. Ltd.
Drogheda Saw Mills Co.

Lord Dunraven
Dublin & Blessington Steam
　　Tramways Co.
Drummond Institute
Dundalk Patent Slip Co.
Dundalk Demesne
　　Brick Works
Dublin Granaries Co. Ltd.
Dublin Hospital
　　Sunday Fund
Dublin Drapers Club

John J. Eyre (Whites Hotel)
Edenderry Spinning Co.

Wm. Findlater & Co.
Ferrier Pollock & Co. Ltd.
Forestbrook Linen Co.
Forrest & Sons Ltd.
D. & T. Fitzgerald

E. G. Gethings & Co.
S. Godkin & Co.
Graves & Co. Ltd.
M. Glynn & Sons
Props. of R. Geoghegan

Bernard Hughes Ltd.
Holmes & Mullin Ltd.
Hunt & Co.
Hamilton Long & Co.
Henry St. Warehouse Co. Ltd.
Hill & Sons Ltd.
Hope Estate
J. H. Hunter & Co. Ltd.
R. & H. Hall Ltd.
Hibernian Plate Glass
　　Insurance Co.
Hickey & Co.
Edward Hughes Decd.

Inglis & Co. Ltd.
Irish Civil Service
　　Building Society
Irish Distressed
　　Ladies Fund
Irish Agricultural
　　Organisation Socy. Ltd.

Irish Ecclesiastical Gazette
Irish Co-operative
　　Newspaper Socy.
Island & Coast Socy. For
　　Ireland

Johnston, Mooney &
　　O'Brien Ltd.
Junior Army & Navy Stores
　　Ltd.
Jervis Street Hospital

Kehoe Donnelly &
　　Pakenham Ltd.
Kelly Dunn & Co. Ltd.
Mrs. J. P. Knox-Gore
Sir E. H. Kinahan Decd.
J. G. King's Estate

Lucan Hydropathic & Spa
　　Hotel Co. Ltd.
Loughrea & Attymon Light
　　Railway
Lane & Phillips
Leopardstown Club Co.
Leinster Club
Lyons Minors
Mrs. Mary C. Livingstone
Little & McClean
Liverpool Warehousing Co.
Limerick Chronicle

Macken Decd.
Gen. W. D. Mears
W. B. Murphy
Thos. McKenzie &
　　Sons Ltd.
Mendicity Institution
McBirney & Co. Ltd.
Meredyth Estates
Rt. Hon. Lord Monteagle
Mining Company of Ireland
　　Ltd.
David Mercier
McEnnery Bros. Ltd.
Mercers Schools
James McCann

W. & S. Mercier
Mrs. Elinor R. Murray
John McBirney & Co.
Mooney Bros.
A. Marsh
David Mitchell
Midland Gt. Western
    Railway Benefit Socy.
Murphy La Couse
P. & T. McGlade and the
    International

P. R. Norton & Co.

O'Kelly Rentals

Phoenix Brewery Co.
Palgrave Murphy & Co.
Pim Bros Ltd.
Ponsonby Rentals
B. Patteson & Co.
Provincial Bank of Ireland
Robert Perry & Son Ltd.
W. M. Patterson & Co.
J. J. Phelps Decd.

M. Rowe & Co.
Robertson Ledlie Ferguson
    & Co. Ltd.
Rotunda Lying-in-Hospital
W. F. Redmond & Co.
Royal Hospital for
    Incurables
Lord Roden
J. N. Russell & Sons
Thos. F. Ruttledge
Laurence Redmond
Ringsend Bottle Co. Ltd.
Roscommon & Leitrim
    Estates
Thos. E. Ryan Decd.
Royal Exchange Hotel
    Co.Ltd.

Southern Hotels Ltd.

Switzer & Co. Ltd.
South Clare Railway Co.
Richard Smith & Co. Ltd.
Daniel Smithwick & Co.
A. H. Smith-Barry
Soldiers Home
E. Smithwick & Sons
Sherrard Smith & Co. Ltd.
Mrs. Sullivan
James Shanks & Co. Ltd.
St. Mark's Hospital
St. Vincent's Hospital
Sackville Street Club
Smyth & Co. Ltd.
Sick & Indigent
    Roomkeepers Socy.
Francis Smyth & Son
R. Hamilton Stubber
Sheridan Club

Exors. Wm. Todd Decd.
Wm. Tempert
Alex Thom & Co. Ltd.
W. & P. Thompson
Henry Thompson & Co.
Turf Club
Tate's Charity

Ulster Manure Co. Ltd.

Victoria Mutual
    Building Society

H. Williams & Co. Ltd.
Waller & Co.
West Clare Railway Co.
Williams & Woods Ltd.
Wicklow Gas Co. Ltd.
Warden Ltd.
Wm. Walker & Son
T. P. Willis
Wynne Rentals
Whiskey Trade Review
Wilson's Hospital
Wynne's Hotel

Appendix 3

THE ALLOCATION OF ROOMS IN 1924

STRUCTURAL ALTERATIONS & ADDITIONS

It is suggested that the work be carried out in the following order:

(1) Build up the doors which lead from the recess on the first floor into Mr. Telford's and Mr. Tulloch's rooms and erect an Enquiry Office on this space. The Cash Boy, who would be installed here, would have complete oversight of every person passing in and out.

(2) Run a counter in Room No. 4 from the door to the window opposite the door. Provide a seat on three sides of the window recess for Callers while the Waiting Room is in use. Let Mr. Tulloch enter his Office through the passage which will thus be provided.

(3) Connect No. 40 with No. 39 by means of an arched opening at the point and on the lines arranged with Mr. Hicks.

(4) As Mr. Gorman, when he called on the 8th ult., stated that he proposed to retain the Caretaker at No. 39, it will be necessary to make such arrangements as will definitely define the respective responsibilities of the Caretakers for the premises on each side of the opening.

(5) Provide a door at the top of the stairs near the Return Room (No. 16) in No. 39 with a view to blocking the exit to Dame Street except for the Caretaker, so that Partners, Staff and Clients will all enter and leave by Trinity Street.

(6) Instal a Public Telephone Exchange in the Enquiry Office with connections to Rooms 2, 3, 4, 5, 7, 8, 9, 17 & 18 and a complete internal telephone system connecting all the rooms with each other, including the Enquiry Office and the Waiting Room . . .

(10) Provide at least one double window in Rooms Nos. 3, 7, and 11 to help to deaden the noise of the traffic.

(11) Extend the Electric Light into the basement and convert all the available accommodation there into strong rooms to correspond as far as possible with the departments upstairs.

ALLOCATION OF ROOMS:

Nos. 40 & 41	Room No.	Allocated to	No. of Persons
First Floor	1	Enquiry Office — Scott; Miss Kinnear; Bertaut; Bryan and Collins	5
	2	Mr. Telford	1
	3	Mr. Tulloch	1
	4	Mr. Brock	1
Second Floor	5	Income Tax	
	6	Missess Webb; Knowles Conby; Graham; Douglas; Bodkin; Ryan; Crawford; Skelton; Smiddy; Sime & Harris	12
	7	Mr. Russell	1
	8	Mr. Shott	1
	9	Mr. Davy	1
	10	Noble; Harding; Speares; Daly; George; Mullen; Knox Fitzgerald; Kerr O'Keefe; Moran; Telford	12
	11	Forsythe; Stafford; Donaldson; Considine; McMeany; Murray; Reid; Neary; Burton; Chambers; Davis	
	12	Colclough; Burke; Crawford; Harris; Hardiman; McCreadie; Woodworth; Fullerton; Durnin; O'Brien and Golding	11
Fourth Floor	13, 14, & 15	Caretaker	
No. 39 Return Room	16	Board Room	
	17	Mr. Mackie	1

First Floor	18	Mr. Wright (with Partitioned off section); Miss Jones; Lynch; Newcombe & O'Kelly		5
Second Floor	19	O'Neill; Graham		2
	20	Slater; Mulligan; Rennix; Howard; Kenny & Crossen		7
				72

Appendix 4

STAFF LIST BY CHARGING GRADE, 1965

Ref. A.[1]

Dempsey,	Des	Egar,	George E.
Elliott,	Bertie	Fitzsimons,	Eddie F.
Luccan,	Aengus	Gallagher,	D. Brendan
MacDermott,	John F.	Garland,	Paddy G.
Manley,	Michael	Hargaden,	Michael F.
O'Leary,	D. Vincent	Hughes,	Tony
Rumball,	Ken J.	Hourihane,	John D.
Wilson,	Des H.	Jermyn,	H. Cecil
		Kelly,	Ian W.
		Mahon,	Henry
Ref. B.		McEvoy,	Seamus P.
Brown,	Alan F.	Meehan,	Tom E.
Bruce,	Martin A.	Molony,	Alan M.
Davis,	James W.	McCabe,	David A. K.

[1] The letters refer to the charging grades, which are detailed on p. 191.

225

Norman,	Ted J.
O'Sullivan,	Ml. Joe
Treacy,	John C.

Ref. C.

Butler,	George E.
Byrne,	Charlie
Dempsey,	Kevin C.
Gallagher,	P. Frank
Graham,	F. James
Grant,	Michael A.
Gully,	Frank M.
Hally,	Des L.
Healy,	Frank J.
Kelleher,	Con A.
Kelley,	John F.
Kelly,	Vincent F. J.
K'Eogh,	John A.
Knox,	Arthur. A
Lucas,	Joe B.
Lyster,	W. Bruce
Mackey,	John
McCarthy,	Frank W.
McDonald,	Pat
McDonnell,	Michael
O'Brien,	Tim V.
O'Broin,	Joe
O'Neill,	P. Hugh
Quill,	Thos. M.
Phelan,	Wm. G.
Partridge,	Ben
Sarratt,	Henry D.
Scorer,	Bill
Scott,	Gerard
Scott,	Bill N.
Waters,	J. Dermot
Wilkinson,	Bill A. H.
Wills,	Dick H.
Young,	Ned R.
Williams,	Glyn

Ref. D.

Donovan,	Thos.
Driver,	T. Owen
Harris,	Miss A.
Houston,	J. C.
Knowles,	Andy S.
Murphy,	Kitt
O'Callaghan,	Paul J.
O'Kennedy,	Oran
O'Rourke,	Frank A.
Rigby,	Emmanuel
Shott,	Jimmy M.
Sweeney,	Dermot

Ref. E.

Adamson,	R. Lindsay
Ball,	Roy
Beahan,	Mrs. L. P.
Bourke,	C. Paddy
Caulfield,	John M.
Devitt,	Tony B.
Dignam,	Miss M. E.
Goulding,	Mrs. E.
Hackett,	Miss C. P.
Jones,	Ml. W.
Keightley,	Miss S.
Keenan,	Barney J.
Keogh,	Eamonn
Kerr,	E. Harry
Kiernan,	Miss M.
MacGuigan,	John M. V.
MacMahon,	Niall J.
Mohan,	Michael T.
Morrogh,	Miss S.
Smyth,	Miss S.
Wilkinson,	Miss G.

226

Ref. F.

Brady,	Miss P.
Butler,	Miss N. J.
Cahill,	Gerry
Clarkin,	Miss R.
Costello,	Miss K.
Coyle,	Paddy N.
Dalton,	Miss E.
D'Arcy,	Denis P.
Davy,	Miss M. A.
Devine,	David J.
Dockery,	Miss E.
Donoghue,	Miss M. P.
Dunkin,	John
Devaney,	Miss M.
Dodd,	Brian
Eyre,	Miss A. P.
Flanagan,	Paddy
Forbes,	James
Galligan,	Miss G.
Heade,	Miss M.
Healy,	Mrs. C.
Hennessy,	Mrs. M. G.
Judge,	Miss G.
Kealy,	Miss C.
Keaney,	Miss M.
Kelly,	John
Kennedy,	Mrs. M.
Knowles,	Miss E. C.
Lane,	David
McGeough,	Miss B.
Mooney,	R. Neil
McCarthy,	Michael
Mitchell,	Seamus
Mahony,	Miss M. V.
Norton,	Kevin
O'Brien,	Miss J.
O'Connell,	Miss M. B.
O'Shea,	Miss K. M.
O'Sullivan,	Miss P.
O'Gorman-Weaver,	Mrs. A
Quinn,	Miss M.
Ryan,	Miss J.
Ryan,	Miss N.
Somers,	Miss C.
Thompson,	Bill C.
Watson,	C. Neil
White,	Miss J.
Wilkinson,	Miss O.
Wood,	Charlie J.
Wood,	Miss K. J. M.

Ref. G.

Atkinson,	Harold
Bailey,	Ken C.
Bartley,	Frank
Boylan,	David M.
Burnett,	David
Burke,	Olaf N.
Cannon,	Sean F.
Collins,	John
Craig,	David G.
Curran,	Ray M.
Dillon,	John B.
Doolin,	Brian S.
Doyle,	Eamonn A.
Douglas,	George
Eason,	David R.
Ellis,	Billy J.
Everard,	Patrick M.
Farrell,	Dick R.
Flanagan,	Seamus
Gairn,	Clive
Gannon,	Tony
Gargan,	David J. E.
Griffith,	Pat
Haddon,	John
Hanan,	W. Roy
Hester,	Pat
Hetherington,	Declan
Hickey,	Neil

Jenkinson,	Tom V.	Ryan,	Derek J.
Jobling-Purser,	Tim E.	Sherlock,	Noel
Keating,	Michael	Slye,	Arthur R.
Keatinge,	Tim W.	Stevenson,	Tim H.
Kenna,	Kevin D.	Smith,	Arnold W.
Kirwan,	Lorcan C.	Taylor,	Malcolm W.
Leeson,	Norman H.	Temple,	Leslie G.
Lynch,	Thomas	Walsh,	Gerald
Mason,	Peter J.	Walsh,	Tim K.
McLoughlin,	Edgar	Watt,	David
McLoughlin,	P. Michael		
Moor,	Michael P.		
Morris,	John		
McCaffrey,	J. J.	**Ref. H.**	
Mooney,	Alan	Coogan,	Mrs. A. P.
Naughton,	Tim I.	Cruise,	Miss. O. M.
O'Brien,	Tim H.	Kelly,	Miss M.
O'Keeffe,	Dan	Kiernan,	Miss R.
O'Neill,	John M.	O'Connor,	Miss M.
O'Sullivan,	David	Richardson,	Miss E.
Pope,	Alan K.		

INDEX

In accordance with modern indexing practices, the names included in the list of partners (see Appendix 1), clients in the late 1890s (see Appendix 2) and staff in 1965 (see Appendix 4) are not included in this index.

Abbey Clothing, 144
Abbey Theatre, Dublin, 98-9
accountancy, 12, 15, 72
    Catholics in, 64-6
    development of, 7, 8, 38, 39-50, 51-3, 128, 171
    and economic growth, 206-7
    hidden reserves, 83, 156
    increasing complexity, 103, 157-8
    and management consultancy, 193-4
    mergers, 207
    and solicitors, 27-8, 33
    and tariffs, 143-4
Accountant, The, 53, 56, 58, 77
accountants
    apprenticeship fees, 130
    English used by Irish firms, 57-8
    examinations, 189-90
    registration of, 136
    role of, 216-7
    status of, 50-9, 90
    training of, 130-2, 189-90
    university graduates, 125, 157-8
Accounting Standards Steering Committee, 206
actuarial science, 132
advertising, 54, 176
    by Brown, Craig & Co., 20
    by Craig & Co., 29
    by Craig Gardner, 56, 215
    by Henry Brown, 13-5
Aer Lingus, 134, 144, 157
Aer Rianta, 171
Agricultural Credit Corporation (ACC), 134, 213
Allan, David, 83, 84
Allan Charlesworth & Co., 84

Allied Irish Banks, 207
Andrews, C. S., 65, 130, 157
Anglo-Irish Free Trade Area, 206
architects, 51
Arnott, Sir John, 46
Arnott's, 30, 32, 41, 45, 46, 74, 103, 136
Arthur Cox & Co., 199
articled clerks, 130-2, 189-90
Arts Club, Dublin, 154
Ashby Staines Brewery, 81
Ashworth Rowan, 209
Atkins, William, 54
Atkins, Chirnside, 54, 217n
Atkins of Cork, 41
Audit Planning Department, 210
audit practice, 207
    Brown, Craig & Co., 17-8
    development of, 39-43, 196
    essay prize on, 41
    importance of, 15, 33, 72, 216
    and junior clerks, 130-2
    state-sponsored bodies, 134-5
    techniques, 158-9, 187-8
    travelling audits, 38-9, 169

back-duty enquiries, 132, 158
Bagnalstown and Wexford Railway, 24
Bagots Hutton, 71
Baker Wardell, 71
Ballymoney, Co. Antrim, 22
Bank of England, 20
Bank of Ireland, 46, 71, 90, 105
    Craig in, 16-7, 31
    merger, 207
    Tulloch director, 155
Bankers' Magazine, 40
banking, 11, 16-7

and accountancy, 40, 90
and Craig Gardner, 134, 155
crisis 1847, 12
mergers, 207
bankruptcy, 7, 12
changes in law, 25
fees, 23-4
see also insolvency practice
Bankruptcy and Insolvency
  Act 1857, 7
Bankruptcy and Insolvency
  Act 1872, 29
Bankruptcy Law and Winding
  Up of Companies Amendment
  Committee, 135
Barings Bank, 71
Beckett, Samuel, 125
Beddy James, 157
Beeston Brewery, 76
Belfast, 15, 124, 208, 209
  Craig Gardner amalgamation, 209
  Craig Gardner income, 80-1, 84, 113, 128, 159
  Craig Gardner partnerships, 141, 178
  first Craig Gardner office, 23
Belfast Bank, 46, 155
Belfast Banking, 74
Belfast Newsletter, 23
Bell laboratories, 194
Benson, Sir Henry, 207-8
Blythe, Ernest, 132
Bodkin, Dr Thomas, 125
Bodkin, Emma, 125
Boileau and Boyd, 75, 101
Boland's Bakery, 46
Bord Fáilte, 144
Bord na Móna, 157
Boycott, Captain, 37
Boylan, P., 154n
Breslin Hotels, 24-5
Brock, Gabriel
  career, 108-9, 113, 135, 153 (p)
  director Provincial Bank, 155
  partner, 133, 141, 163, 170
  President of Institute, 156-7

retires from Craig Gardner, 177, 179
Brooke, Master, 17
Brooks, Maurice, 46
Brooks, Thomas, 24, 89
Brown, Craig & Co., 13-8, 20
  change of offices, 18-9
  insolvency practice, 17-8
Brown, Henry, 10-1, 21, 54
Brown, Reid and Co., 21
brown paper parcel jobs, 131-2
Bruce, David, 18
Brunton William, 20
Buckley, Charles, 141
Buckley, Edward, 80-1, 105-6, 107, 109, 141
Budd, Justice, 200
Builder, The, 18-20
Burke, E. and J., 74, 84
Buttanshaw, Gordon, 177

Cameron, Sir Charles, 66, 67
Cannock's, Limerick, 163-4
Caragh Orphanage, Co. Kildare, 65
Carlton Hotel, London, 81, 83
Carpenter, George Herbert, 103
Carroll, P. J., & Co., 129, 144, 169
Casey and Clay, Solicitors, 29
Castlebellingham and Drogheda
  Brewery, 71
Catholic Church
  and the state, 183-4
Catholic Truth Society, 70
Catholics
  in accountancy, 133-4, 184
  in Craig Gardner, 64-6, 154, 171, 185
  in the professions, 64-5
Censorship Board, 183
Census 1861, 8
Census 1926, 128
Charitable Hospitals (Temporary
  Provisions) Act, 1930, 145
chartered surveyors, 51
Citizens Coronation Committee, 95

230

City of Dublin Hospital, 46
City of Dublin Steampacket
   Co., 135
civil engineers, 51
Civil War, 104-5
Clarence Hotel, Dublin, 131
Clery, Louise, 164
Clery, M. J., 163-4
Clery and Co.
   liquidation, 163-9
Clongowes Wood, 134
Clonmel, Lord, 23
Clontarf, Dublin, 8
Coffey, Gubbins, 217n
Coleman, George, 192-3, 209, 216
Coleman, J. E., 10n
Collins, Michael, 64, 100-1, 102
Companies Act 1862, 39
Companies Act 1963, 193, 196,
   206, 212
company directorships, 176
company launches, 71, 81, 129, 144
company law, 193
compensation claims
   Easter Rising 1916, 103
computerisation, 192
confidentiality, 175-6
Connor, Michael M., 125
Considine, Joseph, 64, 102
Convoy Woollen Company, 41
Coombe Lying-In Hospital, 46
Cooper, William, 65
Cooper & Cooper, 133
Cooper Brothers, 57, 207-8
Coopers & Lybrand, 208
Coras Iompair Eireann (CIE), 24,
   125, 134, 196
   Craig Gardner audit, 172-4
Corinthian Club, 66
corporate business, 80
corporation profits tax, 170
Costello, John A., 178
Cotton, Rev., 65
Court of Bankruptcy, 23-4, 26
   (p), 27-8
Cox, Arthur, 1n, 152
Craig, William Graham, 8

early career, 16-7
earnings of, 23, 27-8
and Henry Brown, 10, 13-5
and Robert Gardner, 21
split from firm, 28-32
Craig & Co., 30
Craig Gardner & Co., 21, 75-7, 89,
   90, 144, 157, 210
   advertising, 56, 215
   amalgamation with Mackies,
      108-9, 113-26
   apprentices, 130-2
   articled clerks, 113, 189-90
   auditing practice, 41-2, 72-4,
      124, 129, 130-2, 187-8, 192, 212
   auditing techniques, 158-9
   Catholics in, 64-5, 154, 171, 184
   and CIE, 172-4
   clients, 23, 24-5, 45-7; see also
      Appendix 2
   ethos of, 175-7
   fee income, 19th c., 22-3, 25, 27,
      32, 38, 43-5, 70-2, 74-5, 84
   fee income, 1900-35, 102, 106,
      113, 128, 141-2, 152, 159
   fee income, 1935-68, 174, 192,
      205, 207, 212, 215
   insolvency practice, 33, 43-5,
      163-9, 196-200
   law cases, 47-50
   London office, 77-80, 81-4
   management consultancy, 193-6
   merger approaches, 207-9
   nationalism in, 100-2
   offices, 79 (p), 114, 212, 213-5;
      see also Appendix 3
   partnership, see Appendix 1
   partnership 1866-75, 22-8
   partnership 1890, 59
   partnership 1903, 84, 92
   partnership 1917, 105-6
   partnership 1924, 109, 141
   partnership 1944, 171, 177, 215
   partnership 1960, 194, 210
   partnership 1971, 215-6
   Protestants in, 133
   reorganisation, 185-9, 209-10

231

salaries, 27, 191-2
secretarial department, 192-3, 212, 213, 216
split, 28-32
staff, 47, 92, 124-5, 128, 186 (p); see also Appendix 4
staff bonus scheme, 106
staff outing, 153-4
and state-sponsored bodies, 134-5
in the Emergency, 169-70
travelling audits, 38-9, 75
in World War I, 100-3
see also Belfast; Coras Iompair Eireann (CIE); Irish Hospital Sweepstakes
Craig Gardner and Harris, 74, 83-4
Crampton, G. and T., 171, 213
Crawford, W., 113
Cream, Mr, 90
Croke, Archbishop, 63
Crosse and Blackwell, 133
Crowe Wilson, 71
Crowley, M., and Co., 108
Crowley, Michael, 72, 93-4, 134
Crowley, Vincent, 93n, 134, 152
Cullen, Louis, 136
Cunningham, John, 27, 54
Cunningham, William, 38-9, 130, 131, 155, 186 (p), 196, 215
  freemason, 70
  partner, 125, 171, 177, 179, 187

Daily Express, 149
Dale, Sarah, 33
Daly and Co., 49-50
Davies, L., 113
Davitt, District Justice, 169n
Davitt, Michael, 37
Davoren, Richard, 47
Davy, Mr, 124
de Paula, Frederick, 158
de Valera, Eamon, 63
debt, imprisonment for, 7, 25
debt collecting, 43
Deloitte, William, 65, 173

Deloitte Plender Griffith, 38, 40, 46, 207
Dempsey, Jerry, 157
'Denis Guiney Saying His Prayers' (Doran), 166-9
Dickens, Charles, 175
Dillon, John Blake, 74n
Dockrell, Thomas, and Co., 75, 76, 89
Donnelly, John, 106, 109
Doran, Mary, 166
double entry bookkeeping, 8, 15
Drogheda Chemicals, 71
Dublin, 9 (p), 15, 37
  population, 8, 12
Dublin Accountants Students Society, 113, 187
Dublin Almanac, 10-1
Dublin and Wicklow Manure Co., 46, 71
Dublin Chamber of Commerce, 136, 177
Dublin City and County Liberal Association, 135
Dublin City Council, 92
Dublin Distillers, 74
Dublin Drapery Warehouse, 163-4
Dublin Gas Independent Consumer's Company, 17
Dublin Stock Exchange, 71, 89, 130, 142, 213
  and ICC, 144
Dublin Theatre Company, 90, 144
Dublin Tram Company, 46
Dublin United Tramways Co. Ltd, 24, 71, 72, 75, 134-5, 172-3
Dublin Whisky Co., 46
Duff, Monica, and Co., 73-4
Duffy, James, 46
Duggan, Richard J., 144-5, 148
Dunbar, McMaster and Co., 14
Duncan, Stan, 196
Dundalk and Newry Steampacket Co., 85
Dundalk Patent Slip Co., 74
Dunlop, 158

Duthie, Mr, 124

Eason, J. C. M., 188
Eason, William Waugh, 103
Eason's, 103-4, 136
Easter Rising, 1916, 103
Economic Development (Whitaker), 179, 183
Economic War, 128
economy, 11, 37
　1920s, 126, 128
　1930s, 141-2
　1950s, 183
　1960s, 205-6
Edward VII, King, 94-5
Electricity Supply Board (ESB), 134, 136
Emergency, the, 159, 163, 174
　fuel shortages, 169
emigration, 183, 205
Encumbered Estates Court, 12
English Institute of Chartered Accountants, 43
Equity and Law Life Assurance Society, 164
Escoffier, Auguste, 81
estate duty, 193
estate management, 16
Eucharistic Congress, 1932, 154
European Economic Community, 206
European Free Trade Area, 206
evictions, 37
examinations, 189-90
excess profits tax, 103, 170

family firms, 185
Farrow's Bank, 213
Ferrier Pollock, 71, 74
Fianna Fáil, 136, 142, 152
Finance, Department of, 179
Findlater, Alex, 33
Findlater, John, 33
Findlater, William, 31, 33
Findlater family, 66
Finnegan, Mr, 76
FitzGerald, Alexis, 178-9

Fitzgerald, D. and T., solicitors, 29
Fitzgerald, Thomas, 54
Freeman, Spencer, 145, 148, 150, 174
Freeman's Journal, The, 46, 135
Freemasonry, 66-7, 70
Fry's, 46
Furniss (clerk), 27

Gaelic League, 63
Gaiety Theatre, Dublin, 98, 99
Gardner, Donnelly & Co., 109
Gardner, John, 47, 54, 55 (p), 80, 84, 92, 100, 109
　as auditor, 73-4
　out of partnership, 106-8
　partner, 59, 105-6
Gardner, Robert, 8, 22, 41, 47, 55 (p), 64-6, 80, 101, 155, 213
　advertisements, 215
　freemason, 67
　income, 33, 70, 76
　knighted, 97
　law cases, 47-50
　and London office, 83-4
　National Assurance Co. report, 89-90
　and Pembroke UDC, 92-7
　remarriage, 33
　retirement, 105
　split with Craig, 28-32
　and the Institute, 54, 57-8
　and William Craig, 21
Gardner House, Ballsbridge, 213-4
Gavan, Duffy, Justice, 165-6
GEC/AEI takeover, 206
Geoghegan, Charles, 20
Geoghegan, T., 188
Geoghegan, Thomas, 134, 213
Gill, M. H., 46
Gladstone, William Ewart, 10
Goulding's, 46
Gracehill, Co. Antrim, 66
Great Famine, the, 11-2
Great Northern Railway, 40, 169
Great Southern and Western

233

Railway, 40
Great Southern Railways, 24, 125, 172-3
Green I.S.L.E. Philately, 198
Gregg, Archbishop, 151
Gregory, Lady, 99
Griffin, 'Mincemeat Joe', 196
Guiney, Denis, 165, 166-9
Guinness's, 46, 57, 136
Gunn, Michael, 98
Guthrie, Edwin, 41

Hallet, Mr, 103
Hally, Des, 157, 199-200
Hamburg-America Shipping, 83, 84
Harris, Allan and Co., 84
Harris, J., 113
Harris, William, 64, 92
    and Craig Gardner, 59, 77-8
    London office, 78, 81, 83
Harry Clarke Studios, 150
Hatry, Clarence, 137, 157
Hayes, William, 11, 157
Hely's, 46
Henderson Brothers, 81
Herapath's Railway Journal, 40
Herbert Park, Dublin, 95-7
Hibernian Bank, 207
Hibernian Plate Glass Insurance Co., 74
hidden reserves, 83, 156
Hill, G. H., 106
Hogan, Daire, 130n
Home Government Association, 25
Home Rule League, 25
Horton, Charles, 67n
Howth, Lord, 23
Hugh Moore and Alexander, 171
Hyde, Douglas, 63

IAOS, 75
In re O'Callaghan, 47, 49
income tax, 10, 103, 129, 184
Incorporated Society of Liverpool Accountants, 52

Independent Newspapers, 144
Industrial Credit Corporation, (ICC), 125, 143, 144, 157
Industrial Development Authority, 178-9
Industry and Commerce, Department of, 143
insider trading, 76
insolvency practice, 7, 29, 33, 192, 196-200
    Brown, Craig & Co., 17-8
    Clery's, 163-9
    Craig Gardner, 23-4, 33, 43-5, 163-9, 196-200
    deregulated, 52
    and the banks, 135
Institute of Chartered Accountants in Ireland, 78, 113, 171
    and advertising, 54, 56
    establishment of, 50-6
    examinations sub-committee, 187
    Fellows of, 108
    Golden Jubilee, 156-7
    inauguration, 21, 31, 46, 54
    office, 213n
    and the Senate, 155-6
    women in, 125
Institute of Chartered Accountants in England and Wales, 53
International Congress of Accountants, 156
International Hotel, 25
Irish Accountants' Society, 133-4
Irish Agricultural Organisation Society, 72n
Irish Banks' Joint Committee, 113
Irish Brewers Association, 144
Irish Cinema, 144
Irish Civil Service Building Society, 74, 75
Irish Commercial and Railway Directory, 29
Irish Hospital Sweepstakes, 101, 102, 124, 135
    and Craig Gardner, 144-52, 187, 192

234

draw ceremonies, 149-50
earnings down, 163
increased competition, 212-3
objections to, 151-2
success of, 147-9
during the Emergency, 174
Irish Independent, The, 135
Irish International Exhibition, 1907, 96-7
Irish Investors Guardian, 76, 83, 85
Irish Law Times, 27-8
Irish Life Assurance Co., 134, 144
Irish Omnibus Company, 125
Irish Provident Assurance Co., 77
Irish Red Cross, 174
Irish Republican Army (IRA), 134
Irish Society of Incorporated Accountants, 45
Irish Sugar Company, 134, 144, 171
Irish Timber Importers Association, 144
Irish Times, The, 46, 94, 97, 105, 178-9, 183-4

Jacob's, 136
Jameson's Distillery, 46
Jervis Street Hospital, 46
Johnston, Jane, 33, 57
Johnston, John Brown, 33
Johnston, Mooney and O'Brien, 46, 56-8, 59, 64, 74, 89, 124
Joint Stock Companies Winding-Up Act 1848-9, 17
joint-stock business, 8
Joyce, James, 85
Junior Army and Navy Stores, 74
Jury's Hotel, 114

Kean & Co., 134
Kean's, 89, 208
Kennedy, Crowley, 134, 144, 152
Kennedy, Mr, 95
Keogh, John, 171
Kevans, Edward, 45
Kevans & Co., 109, 208

Kildare Street Club, 66
King's Hospital, 105
Kinnear, Miss, 122
Knight, W. H., 41
Knights of St Columbanus, 70, 133-4
Kylsant, Lord, 83

land agencies, 7, 16, 23
land agitation, 37
Land Annuities, 142
Land League, 37
Larkin, Michael, 25
Law Society, 51, 130
   Yearbook, 56
Leinster Leader, 65
Lemass, Frank, 134-5, 172
Lemass, Seán, 134, 142, 172
Leo XIII, Pope, 94
Life Association of Scotland Assurance Company, 18
limited companies, 8, 10, 23, 74, 128
   bubble companies, 39-40
   foreign ownership, 143-4
   non-financial, 185
linen companies, 80
Local Government Act, 1898, 92
Locke's Distillery, 174-5
London
   accountancy in, 38, 72
   Barings crisis 1890, 71
   crisis 1847, 12
   and Irish firms, 57-8
   Overend crisis 1866, 20-1
London and Dublin Bank, 12
London Stock Exchange, 207
Lowe, Robson, 200
Lyster, W. B., 206

McBirney and Co. Ltd, 25, 73
McCann, James, 94
McCartney, John, 177, 186(p)
MacDermott, J. F., 188, 190, 194, 210
McEnnery Bros, 76
McGovern, F. J., 41

McGrath, George, 101, 102, 106
McGrath, Joseph, 64, 101, 102, 212
   and Irish Hospital Sweepstakes, 145, 147-8
Mack, David, 130, 215
Mackie, John, 126, 141, 187
   character, 135-6
   and Craig Gardner, 113-24
   memorandum, 114-24, 129
   and Telford, 135-7
Mackie, John, and Co., 108-9, 152
   amalgamation with Craig Gardner, 113-26
Mackie, Johnnie, 135
MacMahon, Noel, 194, 196
McMaster, J. W., 14
McQuaid, Archbishop John Charles, 183
McReadie, C., 113
McSwiney's, 163
management consultancy, 10, 193-6
Manley, Michael, 171
Markievicz, Countess, 99
Marshall Plan, 174
Martin, C. P., 171
Mater Hospital, 145
mergers, 200-1, 207
Metcalf Lilburn Enright, 217n
Miller, Judge, 27-8
Milliken, John A., 177, 199
Moral Rearmament, 154
Moravian Church, 66
Morris, W. O'Connor, 70n
Morrissey, Daniel, 179
Morton, J. R., 177
Muir, Arthur, 156
Mulcahy Redmond & Co., 178
Munster and Leinster Bank, 207

National Assurance Company, 89-90
National Bank, 105, 207
National Loan, 102
National Maternity Hospital, Holles St, 145
nationalism, 63-4, 94-5
   and Craig Gardner & Co., 100-2

Neary, T., 113
Nelson, Jimmy, 178
Nicholson, Charles, 209
Nixon, Sir Christopher, 164, 165-6
Notes on Audit and Accounting Requirements of the Companies Act 1963, 158-9

O'Brien, Gerard, 126, 129-30, 131-2, 136, 176, 186 (p)
   and CIE audit, 172
   partner, 125, 171, 177, 179, 215
   Prices Advisory Body, 170
   Singer liquidation, 199-200
   in UCD, 157, 187, 215
O'Brien, Professor George, 157
O'Callaghan, John, 47, 49
O'Connell, General, 104
O'Connell Bridge, 9 (p)
Official Guide, The, 78
O'Harte, Patrick, 27, 54
O'Higgins, Kevin, 145
O'Neill, W. S., 124
O'Sheehan, Jack, 148n
Overend, Gurney, 20

Palgrave, Murphy, 75
Parker, Alexander, 14
Parkes, J. C., 89
Parnell, Charles Stewart, 37, 63
partners, length of service, *see* Appendix 1
Paterson's, 109
Pembroke, Dublin, 8, 64, 105
   Gardner and the UDC, 92-7
   urban district council, 32-3, 67
Pembroke, Earl of, 32, 93
pension scheme, 190, 192
Peterson Morrison, 208
Phoenix Brewery, 76-7
Phoenix Park assassinations, 37
Pim Bros, 46
Pixley, F. W.
   Auditors: Their Duties and Responsibilities, 41
   Chartered Accountants' Charges, 42-3
poor law, 12

Portmarnock Golf Club, 66, 137
Power-Fardy, R. D., 171
Power's Distillery, 46
Price, Samuel, 65
Price Waterhouse, 40, 141, 172, 194, 196, 209
Prices Advisory Body, 170
Production Engineering, 194
professions, organisations of, 50-2
profit and loss reporting, 193
Profit Sharing and Saving Scheme, 171-2
proportional representation, 135
protectionism, 142-4
Protestants
  in business, 64-6
  in Craig Gardner, 133
Provincial Bank, 46, 155, 177, 207
Purtill, P. J., 156
Purtill's, 134, 171

quality control, 194
Quilter Ball, 40

railway bills, 8
Railway Companies (Accounts and Returns) Act, 1911, 173
railways, 8, 15, 38
  audits, 40, 46, 75
  speculation in, 20-1
Rathmines, Dublin, 8, 32, 64, 92
Rathmines, Rathgar, Roundtown, Rathfarnham and Rathcoole Railway, 24
Rathmines Technical College, 132
rationing, 169-70
Rawlinson, Allen & White, 208
Redbreast Preserving Company, 196
religious discrimination, 64-6, 154, 171, 184-5
Revenue Commissioners, 132
Revenue Commissioners Order, 1923, 117n
Reynolds McCarron, 134, 213
Ringsend Bottle Company, 24
Ritchie, Francis, and Sons, 18
Ritz Hotel, London, 83

Robert Gardner & Co., 29-30
Robinson, Dr Howard, 28, 101, 155-6, 177, 200, 207
Robinson, Heath, 146 (p)
Rotunda Hospital, 46
Royal Bank, 45, 46, 130, 155, 207, 215
Royal Dublin Society, 76
Royal Institute of Chartered Surveyors, 51
Royal Insurance Company, 23
Royal Irish Constabulary, 37
Royal Irish Fisheries Company, 17
Royal Irish Yacht Club, 66
Royal Mail case, 83, 156, 157-8
Royal Marine Hotel, 24
Royal St George Yacht Club, 46, 66
Royal University, 134
Russell, James, 171, 177
Russell, John, 124, 126, 153 (p), 186 (p)
  income, 141
  partner, 108-9, 113, 163, 177, 179

Sackville Street Club, 46
St Lawrence, Lord, 23
salaries, 27, 191-2
Sallins and Baltinglass Railway, 46
Scallan, solicitor, 29
Scotland, 92, 124
Scott, Tom, 104, 122, 154, 172
Scott's Jams, 170
Seanad Eireann, 155-6
secretarial department, Craig Gardner, 18, 192-3, 212, 213, 216
Sedgwick, John, 156
Shanahan's Stamp Auctions, 196-200
Shannon Hydro-electric Scheme, 136
Shott, Eustace, 106, 109, 133, 141, 152, 153 (p), 163, 186 (p)
  Clery's liquidation, 163-9
  death, 178-9
  employment of Catholics, 170-1

freemason, 67, 70
partnership, 177
Sick and Indigent Roomkeepers'
Society, 46-7
Singer, Dr Paul, 196-200
Smith, Hartnell, 172
Smithwick, Daniel, and Co., 46
Society of Incorporated Accountants and Auditors, 53
solicitors, 7, 25, 33, 51, 193
role of, 27-8
staff,
in 1883, 48 (p)
in 1924, see Appendix 3
in 1939, 153 (p)
in 1952, 186 (p)
in 1965, see Appendix 4
state-sponsored bodies, 134-5, 144, 171, 172
Stephen's Green Club, 66
Stewart, David, 124-5
Stewart, Sir James, 13-4, 15
Stokes, Robert, 53
Stokes, Stanley, 156
Stokes Brothers & Pim, 89, 133, 141, 144
accused by Harris, 78
Dunlop accounts, 158
and Institute foundation, 53
size of, 108, 134, 171
Stokes Kennedy Crowley, 93n
Strabane and Letterkenny
Railway, 46
Sunday Pictorial, 174
Supplies, Department of, 163, 164, 169-70
Swift's Hospital, 46
Switzer and Co., 71

tax consultancy, 10, 170, 192, 193, 212, 216
increasing complexity, 157
tax-planning, 163
Taylor, F., 194
Telford, David, 55 (p), 57, 64, 68-9 (p), 101, 118, 121, 123, 153 (p), 176, 177, 213

death, 141, 170
freemason, 66-7
letter to John Gardner, 107
and Mackie, 135-7
and Mackie's, 109, 114
partner, 47, 59, 80, 84, 105-6, 133, 159, 163
religion, 65-6
and Royal Bank, 155
and the Institute, 157
theatrical interests, 90, 97-100, 144
Telford David Cecil, 154-5
Telford, David Jr, 109
Telford, E., 100
Theatre Royal, Dublin, 98, 99
Thom, Alex, and Co., 71, 89
Thompson, McLintock, 155
Thompson, W. & P., 105
Thom's Directory, 7, 13-4, 16, 20, 56
time management, 175
trade, 15-6
development, 205-6
Tramway Construction
Company, 46
Trinity Chambers, Dame St, Dublin, 18
Trinity College, Dublin, 125, 183
Trollope, Anthony, 52
Trotter, William, 124
Tulloch, George Hill, 38-9, 102, 104, 124, 151, 153 (p), 179, 186 (p)
and Bank of Ireland, 155
and Eason's, 103
letter to John Gardner, 107
and Mackie's, 114, 126
and papal flag, 154
partner, 92, 105-6, 109, 141, 159, 163, 170, 175
retirement, 177
and salaries, 176
and the Senate, 155-6
Turf Club, 46
Turf Development Board, 134, 157
Turquand, Young, 57, 92

typhoid outbreak, Pembroke (1878), 33

Unidare, 192
Union Européene des Experts Comptables Economique et Financier (UEC), 206
United Brethren, 66
United Services Club, 46
United Steel Company, 137
University College, Dublin, 125, 157, 187, 215

Victoria, Queen, 64
Voluntary Health Insurance (VHI), 190

Walker, James, 124, 141, 177, 186 (p)
Waterford Glass, 102
Waterhouse, Edwin, 65
Watson, David McCloy, 125, 152, 171, 179, 186 (p), 187, 215
  partner, 177
Webb, Miss, 64
Welsbach Incandescent Company, 81
West Clare Railway, 46, 74, 134
Whelan, Leo, 177
Whinney, Smith and Whinney, 158
Whitaker, T. K., 183
Williams and Woods, 64, 133
Wolfe, Jasper, 132n
women
  in accountancy, 125
Woodington, J. H., and Co., 144
World War I, 100-3
Wright, Archibald, 118, 144

Yeats, W. B., 63

BRANCH
MOUNTJOY PRISON
RAILWAY
CORPORATION CATTLE MARKET
RICHMOND PENITENTIARY
WORKHOUSE
LINEN HALL
VAL MILITARY INFIRMARY
CONYNGHAM ROAD
ROYAL BARRACKS
SMITHFIELD
WESTERN RAILWAY
MERCHANTS QUAY
JAMES STREET
THOMAS STREET
ROYAL HOSPITAL
SOUTH DUBLIN UNION WORKHOUSE
CIRCULAR
PORTOBELLO BARRACKS